CashCow Kids™

CashCow Kids™

The Guide to
Financial Freedom at Any Age!

Lisa Jordan and Sheri Provost

Abacus Publishing, LLC

CashCow Kids™: The Guide to Financial Freedom at Any Age!

Abacus Publishing, LLC
2930 Geer Road, Suite 174
Turlock, CA 95382
Orders@cashcowkids.com
www.cashcowkids.com

ISBN, print ed. 0-9728555-2-1

Published by Abacus Publishing, LLC in association with CashCow Kids™, LLC

CashCow Kids is a trademark of CashCow Kids, LLC

First Printing 2003

Publisher's Cataloging-in-Publication Data
(Provided by Quality Books, Inc.)

Jordan, Lisa.
    CashCow kids: the guide to financial freedom at any age!
/Lisa Jordan and Sheri Provost.
    p. cm.
    Includes index.
    LCCN 2003103388
    ISBN 0-9728555-2-1

    1. Finance, Personal. I. Provost, Sheri.
II. Title.

HG179.J625 2003   332.024
              QBI03-200244

Designed by Peri Poloni, Knockout Books, Cameron Park, CA
Edited by Just Write Literary & Editorial Partners, Keswick, VA

This book is dedicated to
all the parents and kids
searching for the greener pastures
of financial freedom.

Contents

10% of the proceeds
from this book
will be donated to
childrens' charities.

chapter 1

Introduction

"Be Heard, Not Part of the Herd"

· ·

When you turned to this page, did you notice anything out of the ordinary? You probably did a double-take because it looks different from most chapter beginnings. You will soon discover that the notion of looking at things differently is one of the fundamental concepts woven throughout CashCow Kids™. We want you to think "outside the pasture" and open your eyes to practices you can adopt to educate yourself and your kids about money and personal finances.

At CashCow Kids™ our mission is to lead the way in educating both children and parents in the field of family financial literacy. We provide an innovative approach to inspire and challenge families to work together and discover creative methods to increase practical knowledge regarding financial concepts.

Cow Power

Why the theme of cows? Although we measure wealth today by money and assets, not so long ago we measured people's wealth by the cattle they owned. Historically, the cow produced goods such as milk, meat or leather for the owner to trade for some other form of tangible goods. The owner viewed the cow as an income generator.

While our standard of measurement is not exactly the same, the old concept remains. As you read on, we will explain how both you and your kids can develop your own "cash cows."

Security Versus Freedom

In today's society, many people are seeking their own income generators. With financial uncertainty looming everywhere, people from all walks of life are searching for more control. The ideas of job security, safe investments and a sure thing are becoming ideals of the past.

The word *stock,* as in financial stocks and bonds, probably came from the old practice of using cattle or "livestock" as currency.

In Old English, mobile property was called *cwichfeoh,* or "living cattle," while immovable property was referred to as "dead cattle."

Chattel, a term commonly used in today's society, means "non-living personal property." It originated from the dialect word *catel* from Standard English and Old French, which was used to define "wealth."

The Latin word for money, *pecunia,* comes from the old word *pecus,* which means "cattle." That is why at one time the ancient Romans had the image of a bull stamped onto coins.

(Source: *The Complete Cow* by Sara Rath)

In modern society, you generate money in three basic ways. 1) You stay inside your pasture fence and earn your income by *collecting a paycheck.* 2) You decide to venture to other pastures, where there are many options. As a diligent investor, you generate income by *building a portfolio* of paper assets. 3) You also increase income by *investing in passive income-generating opportunities,* such as real estate and businesses.

If you have the right attitude and are equipped with the proper tools, you can find that perfect spot to develop your own cash cow. You can then pass those tools on to your kids. You can shape your family's future and financial success. You can teach your kids the path to financial freedom by helping them create their own opportunities, develop their own money generators and venture into greener pastures. The ultimate goal is to have control over your money and not allow your money to control you.

> ## "Each man is the smith of his own fortune."
> —*Appius Claudius Corcus*

During our preliminary research in writing this book, we surveyed a number of families. We talked with parents and kids of all ages. We gathered some enlightening responses that explained how parents communicate with their kids about such an often-avoided subject.

We also found that once the ice was broken and we were able to introduce the topic of money, both parents and kids were eager to continue the discussion. In fact, many of them sought us out weeks after our initial conversations. Most people wanted to talk about money. The challenge lay in finding just how to go about it. Each generation seems to assume that kids will develop their own money-handling skills without making too many catastrophic mistakes along the way.

How Did You Learn About Money?

Think about how you learned about money management, investing and the whole arena of personal finances. You probably learned either from your parents' actions (more than their words), your teachers' limited classroom offerings or trial and error. This is probably how your parents learned about money, as well.

Our research indicates that for most people this is the way it has always been. Schools throughout the country provide some curriculum on this subject. Yet the material tends to be highly theoretical and lacks hands-on, real-life application. What's more, in a 1997 Liberty Financial Young Investor Survey, teens were asked how they learned about personal finances. Approximately thirty-six percent of the teenagers responded they had "figured it out themselves."

Is the trial-and-error approach working, or is it time you questioned it? Has anyone stopped to teach the next generation about money?

Break The Cycle

We learned from our research that the super-wealthy spend a great deal of their time talking about money and truly educating their children on the subject. Yet the middle class tends to avoid it altogether.

The good news is that each of us has the God-given ability to think independently. You can evaluate ways to change your views and philosophy about money. Now is the time to reevaluate your family's position on financial matters. You have the freedom to break the cycle and raise your kids with new ideas and a fresh outlook.

Unfortunately, it is normal for kids of all ages to continually ask for money and things. From our younger children we often hear the desperate plea, "Mom, can I have a quarter . . . pleeeeeeease!" For many of us, this has become an all-too-familiar mantra that our children repeat every time they pass a bubble gum or bouncy-ball machine.

As our children grow, the mantra matures with them. We begin to miss the days when a quarter would suffice and wonder when we progressed to the era of toys, games and designer clothes. Then the dilemma truly begins. It seems harmless to hand over a quarter or two once in a while. But as the amounts increase, so do our concerns.

How do you help your children break the cycle? Let's face it, that is a question most adults have a hard time answering. Is there more to life than just working, saving and spending? We say there is!

> "Money and success don't change people;
> they merely amplify what is already there."
> —*Will Smith*

Create Opportunities

CashCow Kids™ provides innovative ways to teach children about money yet keep them from becoming obsessed with the stuff. We are not saying abundance is bad. It is what you do with the abundance that matters. In fact, Chapter 9 will inspire you with its true-life stories about kids of all ages who have chosen to give from their abundance.

This book will not merely provide guidelines for children once they have a piggy bank or bank account full of money, although it will do that, too. We provide creative options to help you teach kids of all ages how to generate money, how to view money and how to have that money work for them.

Overview

Each chapter of this book addresses a specific age group, including one just for parents. The chapters are written primarily for adults to read and collect ideas to implement with children. Our intent is to lay a foundation with parents for each phase of growing up. Each chapter discusses key concepts and offers interesting success stories relevant to that age group.

We also identify fun and creative activities, weblinks and practical action items called *Cow Tips*. These ideas are intended to inspire you to interact with your kids to make financial learning opportunities out of everyday events. Your whole family can learn how to make and save money in nontraditional ways and balance the desire to have more money with the importance of sharing with others.

Remember, it's an ongoing educational process for everyone. In each chapter, you will find ideas for *Field Trips*, designed to encourage families to actively broaden their knowledge and understanding of how businesses function in their communities.

Last but not least, each chapter has some fun and humor. We want to help you and your kids recognize both the traditional and nontraditional money-making opportunities available to you. We hope this book will add to your family's financial education and broaden your thinking outside the traditional pasture.

It's a mindset that starts with you.

- ✔ It's not about being a miser with your money.

- ✔ It's not merely about saving your money. Anyone can save, but it does you little good if you don't do anything with your savings.

- ✔ It's about being smart about making money and creating a plan that works for your entire family.

- ✔ It's about having freedom and pursuing dreams.

As a parent, you can be the best example of learning and success. Your family can develop your own unique wealth plan that will have amazing results. As you read on, be prepared to discover new opportunities and graze on them. Every day, you brush up against financial opportunities without even realizing it. The pasture gates that can open are endless. It is learning how to identify and handle those opportunities that will make the difference. Your financial freedom might just be through the next gate.

> "Remember, the door of opportunity knocks every day,
> but the handle does not turn by itself."
>
> —*Anonymous*

Parents

"Old Cows Can Learn New Tricks"

• •

The Money Phases of Parenthood

When our children are babies,
we worry we won't have enough money to buy all the necessities.

When our children are toddlers,
we worry they will put money in their mouths.

When our children attend elementary school,
we try to teach them the value of money.

When our children go to junior high,
we try to limit their spending at the mall.

When our children attend high school,
we want them to learn to make their own money.

When our children are in college,
they never have enough money.

When our children graduate from college,
we ask them for money.

When our children get married,
we worry about how much money the wedding is going to cost.

When our children have babies,
we don't worry about money because we know we can just enjoy
the grandchildren and let their parents worry about the
money phases of parenthood. Our work is done!

You set an example for your children in all aspects of your life. Ideally, you have good solid goals and financial habits already in place for your family. However, if you are like the majority of parents, you are thrilled when you simply get to the end of the day and can say that your kids have managed to wash their faces and brush their teeth before bed.

Parents are continually learning and growing in the position of primary role models. Throughout the remainder of this chapter, we will identify ways you and your kids can grow together. The key point to remember is that their learning and growth starts at home and should be guided by you, their parent.

Calves Follow the Cows

We all have a relationship with money, yet many of us haven't analyzed how we developed it. Where did you first learn about money? Was it something your parents openly discussed with you? Did you learn all you know about money in school? How did you learn what to do with your hard-earned cash? Maybe you are like most people, and each time your income increases, your spending increases, as well. Do your credit cards get more use than your microwave?

We parents often forget that our actions really do speak loudly. Either consciously or subconsciously, our children notice everything we do. For some families, money is a taboo subject. For other families, it is a tool for power and manipulation. And in some families, money is handled and discussed frankly, without a lot of baggage. No matter what your background is, you can learn to reeducate yourself on personal finances and, as a result, teach your children to have a healthy outlook on the topic. One of our goals at CashCow Kids™ is to help your family have control over its money, yet not use money as an instrument of control over others.

Whatever Toots Your Horn (or Rings Your Cowbell)

We all know people who worship money. It controls every aspect of their lives. They know the next big deal is just around the corner and think that as soon as their ship comes in, their lives will be better. Are these people really enjoying life? When they reach their next goal, are they going to be truly happy? Do they have an ultimate goal?

We want to teach our kids to be interested in money and handle it wisely, yet not make acquiring it the driving force in their lives. So keep it simple when giving financial lessons to a child at any age. Even adults get lost when things get too complicated, so for the sake of all involved, simplify, simplify, simplify.

It is important that you give your children the opportunity to deal with money. Throughout this book we will offer simple, age-appropriate ideas that will be a great starting place for you as a family. Make it an ongoing learning experience for the entire herd.

The Calf Fan Club

You are your child's most important advocate. If you as a parent are not supportive of your children in each phase of their lives, who will be? Let your kids know you are their biggest fan.

Emphasize achievements for your entire family and celebrate those achievements, no matter how large or small. There is so much more to life than things. Don't get us wrong. We are not so delusional as to say that money is unimportant. We realize money affects a significant part of what you do every day. Yet we want you and your kids to understand that no matter how much money a person has, money cannot buy everything. Health, happiness and great friends are some of the real treasures in life.

Show Unity Between Both Parents

As in any area of life, it is important to be in agreement with your spouse on the philosophy and handling of money for the herd. Ideally, as a marriage partnership evolves, so does understanding of practical money management.

> "If you don't believe in cooperation,
> look what happens when a car loses one of its wheels."
> —*Anonymous*

We personally are fortunate to have grown together with our husbands in developing our financial strategies. It has been a challenging and, at times, surprisingly pleasant experience.

We realize that showing a united front can be difficult in the best of circumstances. It becomes even more complicated when parents are divorced or separated.

We are not asking you to take a Pollyanna-like view and pretend everything is wonderful all of the time. However, we do suggest you set differences aside and focus on finding a common theme in handling personal finances, regardless of the living situation. If a current or former spouse is completely uncooperative, then the committed parent must strive to deliver a consistent message about money on his or her own. Amazingly enough, kids do remember some of the things we say. So don't give up. Even when it seems that the only one listening to you is your dog.

The best way to develop unity about your financial situation is to take the time to talk as a family about it:

- ✔ **Identify what brings in money for you each month. This is an asset. An asset is any positive cash flow item.**

- ✔ **Identify what costs you money every month. This is a liability. A liability is any negative cash flow item.**

- ✔ **Do you need to consider new financial options?**

- ✔ **Do you allocate money to savings each month? Saving is not the ultimate goal. Yet, for those who wish to get their money working for them, this habit will be crucial.**

- ✔ **Keep your personal financial statement up to date.**

- ✔ **Create a wealth plan. A wealth plan is a plan to build or increase your sources of income. Research ways you can make money. Develop a plan to get your money working for you.**

- ✔ **Have an end plan. Know your limits, your goals and when and how you will move on to the next opportunity.**

Only you can determine what is best for your situation. It takes time, thought, lots of discussion and some homework on your part. Most of all, it takes agreement from all parties involved.

Talk, Talk, Talk

While it may be true that actions speak louder than words, your words are still important. Be open with your kids. Take advantage of opportunities to talk with them about the many aspects of money. There are so many situations you can use as good examples to initiate conversations. These talks can spur discussion about money, how to make it, how to spend it and how to use it to its fullest potential.

> "If you want to become rich, start investing a lot of time
> before you invest a lot of money."
> —*Robert Kiyosaki*

Discussions can also generate great business ideas or at least get your kids thinking about the many different types of businesses that exist. Evaluate why they exist, how they exist, who they depend upon, why they are successful and who is running them.

Whenever appropriate, talk with your kids about how you spend your money and where your money comes from. Does your household have one primary source of income or multiple streams of income? Do your kids even know what you do to earn money? Are they aware of your employment and educational background? Do they know why you chose to go into the type of business or occupation you're in? Do you? Tell them the pluses and minuses of your business. Use this opportunity to be open with your kids. By beginning the discussion of business opportunities while they are young, you will allow your kids to observe and learn about businesses as they grow.

The following is a list of discussion ideas to spur conversations about money. This list is just the tip of the iceberg. Once you get going on a topic, many more possibilities can be pursued. A more complete list of talking points is identified in Appendix B.

At Meal Time **. . .** Where did the food come from? Where did you buy it? Who grew/produced the food? Who delivered the food to the store? Identify all the different types of businesses it took to get your food on the table. Discuss the jobs of friends or family members who work in food-related industries.

19

Warehouse Shopping . . . Large discount warehouse stores provide the perfect opportunity to talk with your kids about money. Is shopping there really such a good deal? Do people believe they are getting a deal simply because the items are sold in large quantities in a big warehouse? Let them do some calculations and figure it out. Have them identify how much of the stuff you buy at these stores are necessities and how much are just "I wants." There is nothing wrong with "I wants," yet it is important to differentiate between wants and true needs.

Television Time . . . The commercials during your TV time with the kids provide a natural segue to discussing money-related topics. Talk about the product for sale, the marketing of the product, and all the people and businesses related to that one product. Help them learn to be thinkers, not just little sponges. (Hint: To prevent overkill and maintain open communication, avoid analyzing *every* commercial, *each* time you watch television with your kids.)

Family Meetings . . . Create family unity. Hold regular family meetings to discuss important financial business. Identify a standing time for all family members to be present. You can discuss budget issues, clothing funds, allowances (if applicable), vacation plans, why the family is cutting back in certain areas, investment opportunities and so on. This is a great time to identify goals and work together as a family while developing support for one another in individual endeavors.

> "Rich people plan for four generations.
> Poor people plan for Saturday night."
> —*Gloria Steinem*

Grandparents/Elderly . . . After you have visited with grandparents or elderly friends, talk to your kids about the concept of retirement. What does retirement mean? How do retired people live if they aren't actively working? What enabled them to earn money so they could retire? Remind them that retirement does not have to occur when a person is sixty-five. Discuss why some people are able to retire much earlier. What does it take to be "financially free" at any age? This should be a huge area of focus. (Hint: It *is* possible to be financially free at any age!)

Allowances . . . The A-word debate goes on: "Should we or should we not give our kids an allowance?" Many generations of parents have struggled with this age-old question. We are not here to tell you what you should do about the allowance issue. You must decide what is right for your situation. We do feel that that there should be some type of mechanism where your child can learn about handling money, managing it and becoming educated about the responsibility that goes along with possessing it. If you do decide to give allowances, remember to discuss the guidelines, if any, for spending the money. Good foundational principles for saving and spending are identified in chapters 3 and 4.

Credit Cards . . . The issue of credit and debt can be a mystery to kids if they don't truly understand how it works. Start talking with them at a young age to help them understand how a credit card can be both useful and at times, detrimental to their overall finances. Handing over credit cards to young kids can be dangerous. Yet, when they're old enough, let your kids learn through some real life trial and error. Don't make the mistake of bailing your kids out if they over-spend. What lesson would you be teaching them then?

> "There is no dignity quite so impressive,
> and no independence quite so important, as living
> within your means."
> —*Calvin Coolidge*

Game Night . . . Robert Kiyosaki, in his book *Rich Dad, Poor Dad (Tech Press, 1997)*, talks about how, as a young boy, he loved to play the game Monopoly. He and his friends played this game frequently, while his rich dad played it in real life. This game teaches great financial principles and allows families to learn in the generally relaxed setting of playing a game. We agree that games are a great teaching tool. The original Monopoly®, Monopoly Jr.® and the new CASHFLOW® games (created by Kiyosaki) will accommodate all age groups.

Discuss the parallels these games have to the real world. How does investing in real estate make your money work for you? What are some other ways a person can make money outside of a traditional work environment?

What are the pros and cons of this kind of investment? The goal is to help make teaching financial lessons as fun and pain-free as possible.

Games that promote financial learning:

- ✔ **Monopoly**®
- ✔ **Monopoly Jr.**®
- ✔ **Life**®
- ✔ **Payday**®
- ✔ **CASHFLOW for Kids**™
- ✔ **CASHFLOW 101**®

Live Below Your Means

Every household struggles with the temptation to increase spending as earnings increase. When your household starts making more money, are you tempted to go out and buy that new car or upgrade into a bigger, fancier house? It is human nature to want to keep up with the Joneses next door, but avoid that. The Joneses may look like they have it all together, but they may be up to their eyeballs in debt and regretting it every single month.

Ultimately, we as parents want to teach our children to be financial achievers, not mega-consumers. Our goal should be to show our kids that we don't make money so we can just spend more. Teach this to your kids by living it.

Allow Children To Experience Failure

Failure is difficult for anyone at any age. Although it is hard as parents to allow children to fail, it's in their best interest if you allow your kids to make mistakes. And when they happen, don't make their mistakes into monumental events; instead, help your kids *learn from them*. That is the key. In fact, if handled correctly, mistakes can be the absolute best way to learn and grow.

Remember to be sensitive to the individual and the circumstances. At times, discussion can facilitate learning, yet frequently the experience itself will be the best teacher if you handle the situation well. Just remember to support your kids and be available to them, even if they don't seem very receptive. In the end, your love and support will be the best catalyst for learning and growth.

On the flip side, many parents are too quick to bail their children out of financial woes. Kids do not learn their lessons if the problem is solved without any consequences. The connection between their actions and the repercussions is necessary for their learning. If your young calf unwisely spends his entire weekly allowance on concert tickets without saving a penny for the necessities he is required to buy, don't bail him out. Let him learn from his poor decision the hard way: It's doubtful he will forget the experience.

While you are teaching children responsibility and all of that other good stuff (that they dread), it is important not to put unrealistic expectations on them. Let them be the goofy, energetic kids they are. They are going to make mistakes at one point or another. Why not let them make quite a few while they are still living under your roof and you can be there to help them or at least to listen? Why not let them see that when they make mistakes, they have the ability to learn from them?

When Wrong Is Right

Occasionally, our families have a "Wrong Answer" day where we all have fun giving wrong answers to nutty questions. We perfectionists find that it helps all of us lighten up a little. In addition, the game demonstrates that it is okay to be wrong and that we can learn from our mistakes. Several possible questions:

1. **When driving: Which way did I just turn?**

2. **When grocery shopping: How many gallons of milk should I buy?**

3. **What color was that spaceship that just flew through your room?**

4. **What type of pizza do you want from Taco Bell?**

The objective of this game is to let kids choose some of their own questions, which can be silly, outrageous and sometimes enlightening. Of course, the teachers at school probably won't appreciate this game, so help little ones understand this is a special game for the family. We doubt if they'll give credit for wrong answers in the classroom or on a test. The whole idea is to encourage learning from a fun, new perspective.

If Abraham Lincoln had been afraid of failure, he would have never become president of the United States. His life is a remarkable story of a man who experienced setbacks many times but kept rising to the occasion. Each time he failed, he moved on and eventually achieved his goal. In the process he gained the respect and admiration of many people and nations.

Abraham Lincoln . . .

- ✔ **failed in business at age twenty-two,**
- ✔ **was defeated in a run for the state legislature at age twenty-three,**
- ✔ **failed in business at age twenty-five,**
- ✔ **coped with the death of his sweetheart at age twenty-six,**
- ✔ **suffered a nervous breakdown at age twenty-seven,**
- ✔ **was defeated in a run for speaker at age twenty-nine,**
- ✔ **was defeated in a congressional nomination at age thirty-four,**
- ✔ **was elected to Congress at age thirty-seven,**
- ✔ **lost renomination for Congress at age thirty-nine,**
- ✔ **was defeated for the Senate at age forty-six,**
- ✔ **was defeated for the vice-presidency of the United States at age forty-seven,**
- ✔ **was finally elected president of the United States at the age of fifty-one, and**
- ✔ **is remembered as one of the greatest leaders Americans have ever had.**

Persevere as a parent and teach your kids to go for their dreams. If quitting isn't in their experience, they won't think of it as an option.

Allow Children To Explore Their Passions

Each one of us has individual passions, whether we think of them in that way or not. Your passion could be painting, writing, music, cars, sports—the list is nearly endless. Your kids are beginning to discover their interests and passions, as well. No matter what their passions are, help nurture and develop them in some way.

Of course, life does have its more realistic side. Whether they like it or not, your kids will need to grow up and find their own way to earn a living, pay the bills and complete a myriad of necessary daily tasks. Yet, no matter what their passions are, you can help them find ways to pursue them and experience all they can become.

> **Field Trip Idea:**
> ## Spa Day
> **Parents:** Take a trip (without the kids) to a local spa or hotel and experience how just a little bit of money can buy you a lot of rest, relaxation, peace and quiet.

One of the best rewards of being a parent is to see the unbridled spirit of a child. There are no boundaries. Their imagination is endless with enthusiasm for all of life. They just know there are no mountains they cannot conquer.

The last thing we want to do as parents is squelch that spirit. In fact, most adults could use a good dose of that spirit to rekindle their desire to achieve their own dreams. Early in their lives, children have no fear, yet adults tend to live in fear. Fear of what? Fear of failure? Fear of being different? Fear of being laughed at? Just what are we afraid of?

It's amazing what people won't try. Before kids start developing a sense of fear, allow them the freedom to pursue their interests. We can almost guarantee that these interests will change over the years, but the accumulation of all their experiences will enrich them. It is the freedom to pursue a dream that can make dreams become reality.

We have some close friends who have two teenage daughters who are novice artists. The girls are quite talented and enjoy painting and drawing in all media. When the family was planning a big party for one of the girls' sixteenth birthday, the parents gave the okay for the girls to express their talents. They transformed their entire house into a nautical-themed cruise ship, painting several walls with landscape and ocean scenes that looked like postcards.

Their parents could have not allowed them to go quite that far with the project. Instead, they allowed their daughters to pursue their passion and express their talents through their artwork on the walls of their home. This is merely an example of what worked for one family. You'll know when to let your children take the ball and run with it. Remain open and willing to help them explore spreading their wings to full span.

> ## "Parents can tell but never teach,
> ## unless they practice what they preach."
> —Arnold Glasow

Continue Learning

A common attribute you will find in most successful people is an open mind. The desire to learn new ideas, concepts and philosophies, and have untraditional thoughts is unusual. Most people want to continue in the same way because it is comfortable. We often seek security over all else. We are creatures of habit.

If someone doesn't see things the same way as you do, can you relate to them? Do you even want to try? Do not be closed-minded. You will rob yourself of a richer, fuller life than you could have ever dreamed. Allow your kids to see that you are continually learning new things and are even open to ideas from them.

Financial success can arise from the willingness to learn. Try to learn something new each and every day. If you are constantly learning new things, new ideas will constantly be stimulating your brain. First and fore-most, the stimulation will always keep you youthful. Second, you never know what whiz-bang idea can evolve from what initially seemed like just another crazy scheme.

Some practical ways to continue learning:

- ✔ **Play challenging board games, such as chess.**
- ✔ **Read a newspaper daily.**

- ✔ Subscribe to a new magazine.
- ✔ Write a story.
- ✔ Paint a picture.
- ✔ Visit a museum.
- ✔ Laugh.
- ✔ Attend a play.
- ✔ Start a debate at the dinner table.
- ✔ Have stimulating conversations with friends.
- ✔ Go to a planetarium.
- ✔ Attend a lecture at your local university.
- ✔ Go to the library regularly.
- ✔ Learn a new sport.

Conclusion

Remember, money cannot guarantee happiness, yet it can give you the freedom to make the choices you want. It is your job as a parent to educate, motivate and empower your children with the proper financial tools to succeed in life. The best foundation in teaching your kids about money is to model a lifestyle based on solid financial principles. It is much easier to make sound choices when money isn't the dictating factor in your life. The proper perspective on money can allow you and your family to concentrate on the things that really matter.

1. Be your children's biggest fan:

    ✔ Give them encouraging words daily.

    ✔ Be supportive of new ideas.

    ✔ Encourage their interests and dreams.

2. Determine the best mechanism for your family to teach your kids how to handle and deal with money.

3. When appropriate, seek input from each family member as you develop your family's philosophy on money.

4. Use positive language when discussing financial topics with your family.

5. Continue learning with an open mind.

    ✔ Read or listen to one book a month on a money-related topic.

    ✔ Subscribe to a financial newspaper.

    ✔ Take a real estate course or seminar.

    ✔ Take a course on a subject you know nothing about.

6. Keep some type of money or financial tapes/CDs in your car in case you get stuck in traffic.

7. Reevaluate your family's formula for financial success on a regular basis.

8. Seek opportunities to talk with your kids about some aspect of money or finances.

9. Hold regular family meetings to discuss money issues, investments, wealth plans, etc.

10. Play fun financial-based games together regularly.

11. Establish a policy regarding borrowing money within the family.

chapter

Preschool

"From Piggy Banks to CashCows"

• •

Hey diddle diddle
The piggy bank whistled
The cow jumped over the dime
The little kids laughed to see such fun
And the dollar ran away from time.

As a rule, preschoolers do not understand the value of money. Kids know coins are special, but why? They see that they are silver and shiny. By age three, much to their parents' dismay, most kids have discovered that coins taste yucky. Yet for some reason they still treasure them. That's where you come in. You set the standard by your words and actions for how they will initially view money.

As children grow, they begin to realize they can use money to buy fun "stuff." Yet the value of different currency or coins is generally still a mystery. They think that because a nickel is bigger than a dime, the nickel is better. One of our son's favorite tricks is to trade his big nickels for his younger sisters' little dimes. The girls think they are getting a great deal. It takes a lot of explaining to get them to give up their huge nickels and take back their little dimes.

In some ways, we set our preschoolers up for confusion. They have just grown out of the stage when they put everything into their mouths. Understandably, parents try to keep coins out of their sticky little hands. Then suddenly the financial world opens up to them. Mom is no longer taking their treasures away; she is actually giving them quarters to hold for their very own.

Moooolah

Depending on your personal preference, you may or may not want your young children to handle money. Taking your children's personalities and proclivities into consideration, it is generally a good idea to start teaching your kids about money when they begin to show an interest in it. If you handle this subject correctly, your children eventually figure out that the little dime is actually worth more than the big nickel.

We recently heard a good idea from a friend. When Dad gets home, he empties the change from his pockets. Then he and his son put the money in a special bank. They count the money and talk about the names for the different coins. This is a fun time for both and really helps the child to become more familiar with the various coins.

Here, Piggy Piggy

There are all kinds of banks available. Choose one that is fun for your child. There is the famous piggy bank, the princess bank, the superhero bank, and the always-useful big jar. The point is to make saving money fun for your children.

One of the best resources we have found for locating banks is on the Internet. In Appendix D at the end of this book, we list many websites we found helpful in locating banks for children.

CashCow Kids™ offers our own trademark CashCow Bank. This bank has three slots, one for paying yourself (saving), one for spending and another slot for giving. The concept behind this bank is to teach kids to save appropriately. Don't we all wish we had the advantage of learning this concept at such a young age? This bank is available on our website at **www.cashcowkids.com.**

It is also enjoyable for children to make their own banks. Household products that make fun homemade banks:

1. *Coffee cans.* **Let them decorate the cans with paper, stickers, jiggly eyes or felt. It will allow them to be actively involved, and they will love to show off their creations.**

2. *Water bottles* **(plastic). These are fun because the kids can look right into the bottle to see how much money they are saving. Be careful not to fill them too full, though; they can become quite heavy.**

3. *Shoe boxes.* **As with coffee cans, these are fun for kids to decorate. Their advantage over coffee cans is that they are easier to paint.**

4. *Milk cartons.* **If you like the idea of the three compartments in your savings plan, take three milk cartons and glue them together (side by side). Cut slots in the top of each carton. Your kids can paint or decorate them like houses, a farm or whatever they wish.**

Whether or not you decide to give your children an allowance, you might consider giving them small amounts of money every once in a while. This provides another useful opportunity for them to learn about and become familiar with money. For

During World War II, the U.S. needed the copper from pennies to make communications equipment. As a result, pennies began to be made of steel.

The rare 1943 copper-alloy cent is one of the most sought-after items by coin collectors. Only about forty 1943 copper pennies were minted because of the war restrictions.

The way to find out if your 1943 penny is copper is with a magnet. If you can't pick it up with a magnet, it's copper, and it could be worth a lot of money!

A 1943 copper penny was auctioned off on December 22, 1999 for $112,500.

Source: www.thinkquest.org

example, try giving them fifty cents each week. One week you could give them two quarters, another week five dimes, the next ten nickels, the next fifty pennies and so on. Just let them know that each time they are still getting fifty cents. This will help lay the foundation for the values associated with the different coins.

The following ideas will give preschoolers the opportunity to earn a little bit of money for special things:

- ✔ **Recycle soda cans from home or a parent's office.**

- ✔ **Help grandparents pull weeds. (Just make sure youngsters are very closely supervised, or those beautiful tulips will disappear, as well!)**

- ✔ **Help clean out the car. (Be careful with this one. When a friend's son was five she let him have a penny for every piece of garbage that he brought to her. He proceeded to tear up every piece of paper he found. That penny apiece turned into at least a dime every time!)**

- ✔ **Gather the family's dirty laundry. Sort into piles according to color.**

- ✔ **Dust and clean mirrors and television sets. Kids this age love to use squirt bottles. Parents will need to monitor their little helpers to ensure the mirrors aren't getting too clean!**

- ✔ **Help bring in the groceries.**

- ✔ **Help empty the dishwasher.**

- ✔ **Help empty wastebaskets throughout the house.**

Playtime

As your children grow older, they will quickly start grasping the concept of what money is. Another great way to reinforce this is to introduce sorting games early on. If you do not want your kids to handle real coins, the pre-made "fake money" games are ideal. These can be found at most educational stores as well as many large chain discount stores.

Play sets we found online for preschoolers:

> ✔ CatalogCity.com has coins in a bank set.

> ✔ HeatherEducational.com also has a play set for little bankers. It includes a checkbook with checks, deposit and withdrawal slips, passbook, play cash card, receipt stamp, bills and plastic coins, along with suggested activities.

If you want to make your own, you can make little banker sets out of colored paper and pens. Yet children often like to play with the real thing. If you are worried about germs, wash up a cup full of coins and let them at it. Then they can sort out all of the pennies, nickels, dimes and quarters. Coin identification comes easy with repetition. Before you know it, they will be experts on the stuff.

> ## "In the book of life, the answers aren't in the back."
> —Charlie Brown (Charles Schultz)

Another great way to help children get comfortable with coins is to let them use them to buy things.

Some ideas:

> ✔ Buy stamps from the machine at the post office.

> ✔ Buy a newspaper for mom or dad.

> ✔ Buy food or sodas from a vending machine.

> ✔ Buy bubble gum.

> ✔ Pay for their ride at the grocery store.

> ✔ Pay for their own treat at the store, separate from the groceries.

> ✔ Take their own money to give at church.

> ✔ Give money to the Salvation Army bell ringers.

> ✔ Put coins into the parking meter.

Field Trip Idea:

Fast Food Restaurant

Talk with the manager to set up a tour of a mainstream fast food restaurant. Take the kids to see the behind-the-scenes workings of the operation.

- Notice who the restaurant serves.

- What other amenities does the restaurant have?

- Does it have a playground, vending machines or video games? Why would the restaurant have these things?

- Does the restaurant serve a "kid's meal"?

- What is the free toy in the "kid's meal"?

It is important to keep an open dialogue with kids about money yet not make more of it than is necessary. Money is not, and should not, be the focus of preschool years. Dirt and dolls are more important to most children at this age. Fun and games are the rule of the day. Therefore, throughout this book we will continue to give you ideas to make handling and learning about money fun and interactive.

Punishment?

While most of us did not acquire a vast amount of financial knowledge when we were this age, it is not too early to begin to teach our children. Richard K. Anderson, Jr. is an example of a child who began his financial education at an early age. When he was three years old, his father punished him for bad behavior by making him watch CNBC instead of cartoons. This punishment became a teaching tool. Richard was fascinated with the stock market and began learning about it. At the age of five, young Richard made history as the youngest person ever to ring the opening bell of the New York Stock Exchange. That same day, the official exchange chairman, Richard Grasso, appointed him chairman for a day after he became aware of Richard's knowledge of stock market history.

"The creation of a thousand forests is in a single acorn."

—Anonymoous

While we may not choose to have our children watch CNBC on a daily basis, this story (Africana.com) is a good example of how early financial education can influence even the youngest of children. We are sure Richard's father provided an example for him by watching the news with him. This reminds us that at every age, it is good to teach by example.

If you prefer to portray financial lessons in a simpler manner, show your children how you are saving for your vacation, a certain piece of furniture or future investment. Let them see that you do not just go out and buy anything you want, whenever you want it. Children especially enjoy helping you save for a family-related purchase or event, something they will get to use or be involved in.

Saving

We are currently saving for patio furniture. Our children are able to see that we do not just go out and buy everything immediately. We check the store weekly to see if the furniture has gone on sale. They love to run to the back of the store and see if there are any sale signs up. It has been a good lesson for them to see the money grow in our "water bottle" bank. They can't wait until we have enough saved and can actually bring the furniture home.

Most kids have a hard time learning patience. We live in a society that constantly illustrates instant results. On a child's level, they see microwave popcorn and fast food restaurants. Why should they have to wait for anything? If you can at least begin to teach your children the value of delayed gratification now, you will be laying a very strong foundation for their future that will have amazing results throughout their lifetimes. Yet you may wonder, in today's environment, how you can teach your children that waiting can actually be a good thing.

Delayed Gratification

A friend recently told us a story about how her husband helped their son learn to wait for a better reward. Their son, Seth, was having a particularly difficult time attending a day camp that, earlier in the summer, he had begged to attend. From prior experience, they knew that once Seth got involved with his friends at the day camp (which lasted only three hours a day), he would overcome his shyness and have a ball. So they made a deal. Each morning Seth attended day camp, his dad would give him a small pack of trading cards worth about one dollar. But, if Seth would attend camp the whole week and wait until the end of the week to receive his cards, his dad would buy him the super pack of trading cards worth about ten dollars. Therefore, it was either cards worth a buck if he bought them each day or cards worth ten smackers if he waited until the end of the week to buy them.

Guess what he chose? He wanted the one-dollar cards. Seth wanted to be able to get the cards immediately each day after camp ended. At this point, the dad was a little frustrated. His great plan to teach his son the rewards of waiting for something better was not working. So he took Seth to the store and showed him the difference between the small and large pack. After thinking it over, Seth chose the large pack. They immediately purchased it, took it home and put it on top of the refrigerator to open at the end of the week.

It was a good lesson for all. Our friend told us that she was frustrated with her husband at first. She told him, "That's not a good lesson; you already bought the cards for him." Her husband was more realistic. His goal was not to see how difficult he could make this decision for Seth. He wanted to show him that waiting can sometimes pay off. Seeing the box on the refrigerator every day was a huge motivation for Seth. By the end of the week, he was so excited to open that box of cards that he could not wait to attend the last day of camp. He actually enjoyed camp and was glad he had waited for the larger box of cards. Our friend admitted that her husband had been right to give him the visual motivation to wait for the bigger prize.

One of the reasons we challenge you to introduce lessons about money early on is to help keep it in its proper perspective. It may seem that we are doing just the opposite, but we are not encouraging you to raise money-obsessed kids. This is the age where you will start to lay the foundation. You want them to learn about the value of money.

"If you want a kitten, start out by asking for a horse."

—Naomi, age 15

1. Whatever age an ordinary child starts asking about money is the time you turn an ordinary little child into a money-smart kid.

2. Start your child saving in some kind of bank *today!* Even if it is just pennies to begin with, the concept of saving will start to stick. Talk about the three categories of saving, spending and giving.

3. TV time is a great time to talk to your kids about commercials and all the things they "want." It is good for kids to get used to hearing "no" answers with explanations that they will not immediately get everything they ask for—not even close. They need to begin to learn delayed gratification (of course, they won't fully grasp it until a later age).

4. Observe what television shows your children watch. Does any of their television viewing time increase their financial education?

5. When your child asks to buy an item at the store, explain why you're not going to buy it right now. Discuss how you choose to use your money for something bigger they can understand. (In time this does work, but it takes consistency.)

6. Game idea: Paste or tape coins on index cards. Write the name of the coin on the back and the amount the coin is worth. This will help your kids learn the names of the coins as well as their value. Parents, quiz your kids and let them quiz you. Kids love to pretend to be the teacher.

7. Research websites that provide fun money games for kids this age. Several are listed in Appendix D, but many more exist.

Kindergarten to Third Grade
"Chew Your Cud"

∙∙∙

Knock, knock!
Who's there?
Orange?
Orange who?
Orange you gonna buy me a toy?

Recently, we made an alarming discovery about our families. Our kids have developed a serious case of the dreaded disease known as "toy-i-tis." Our families have somehow accumulated enough toys to fill at least one landfill, maybe two. We have Dollar Store toys, kid's meal toys, toys received as gifts, toys from garage sales and (although we're a little embarrassed to admit it) toys our sweet angels conned us into buying in weak moments of shopping exhaustion.

One of the authors often suffers from shopping exhaustion because she has an unusual problem, foreign to most women: She hates to go shopping. She fears there is no cure. She has tried taking a highly organized list, shopping with friends and even shopping alone. Nothing works.

Last Mother's Day, her husband attempted a drastic treatment. He sent her to the mall, armed with some cash and the following orders: "Go and buy yourself something. Here is my cell phone. Don't bother calling unless you have spent all of the money on yourself. Until then, I will not come and get you." Sadly, two hours later, she called to update him on her progress. Zilch. Zero. Nothing. She could not find a single thing. Her husband was understandably frustrated (as much because the kids were climbing the walls as because she had made no progress). She took the hint and after another three hours, she eventually managed to buy a couple of outfits.

Cowlection of Stuff

One would think that the children of a woman with such stunted shopping habits would live simple lives. However, like many children, hers have been "blessed" with an abundance of stuff. Part of the toy dilemma lies in her kids, who intuitively sense her weakness and prey upon her desire to get in and out of the store as quickly as possible. The other possible reason for their vast accumulation is that friends and relatives have a healthy love of shopping and generously share their bounty with them.

How does such a family cure themselves? Is there any hope for them? Thankfully there is. They set limits. Part of this solution came naturally. They simply refused to move into a larger home just to house an ever-expanding toy collection. (The only other option was to turn the garage into toy central. The father, understandably, refused to give up his domain.)

They decided how many toys they were going to allow in the household. Then they set up a few rules for adding new toys to the collection. Whenever someone wanted a new toy or book, they either sold or gave away two toys/books. This solution solved many problems at once. The accumulation of toys decreased while their children learned to value both their new toys and the ones they already had.

Cow-workers

No matter how much or little money your family currently has, it is imperative that your kids learn a good work ethic. We all know people who were pampered and catered to all their lives. When they reached adulthood, they seemed to have a difficult time coping with responsibilities. Don't cheat your kids out of this fundamental key to success. No matter what they decide to pursue, they can accomplish it with hard work and discipline.

Our families' prescription for instilling a work ethic is a "job jar." We set up the jar for projects we are willing to pay our children to complete. Each week we cut up squares of paper and write jobs on them. We fold them up and put them in the job jar. After the kids finish their daily household chores, they can earn a little extra money by picking a job out of the jar. We do not pay them for making their bed, cleaning their rooms or feeding their pets. Paying jobs are over and above their normal daily routine.

Some job jar ideas for this age group:

- ✔ **Sweeping the porch, deck, driveway**
- ✔ **Pulling weeds (in clearly defined areas)**
- ✔ **Washing windows (with supervision, depending on age)**
- ✔ **Vacuuming**
- ✔ **Watering outside plants (a family favorite)**
- ✔ **Straightening and dusting bookshelves**
- ✔ **Folding laundry**
- ✔ **Raking leaves**
- ✔ **Cleaning up after pets**
- ✔ **Helping to empty the dishwasher**
- ✔ **Arranging refrigerator pictures/magnets**
- ✔ **Helping to remove bed sheets**
- ✔ **Putting away clean laundry**

The money they earn from these special jobs can be spent however they like. One author's son initially spent this money as fast as he could earn it. He soon began to realize that if he saved some of it, he could buy an even "better" toy later on. He also started being more cautious about how he

Field Trip Idea:

Unique Business

Go visit a super deluxe pizza parlor with cool video games, bright lights, loud music, kiddie rides, etc.

Discuss:

- **How many quarters per day go into those machines?**

- **How many machines are there?**

- **What attraction is your kid's favorite?**

- **Which game or ride costs the most?**

- **What did you dare eat?**

- **What were the most useful prizes that you came home with?**

spent his money. Now, he has an eagle eye for sale tags at Wal-Mart, and when spending *his* money he constantly checks the clearance aisle. He also takes better care of the toys he buys. Encouraging a little hard work can teach a lot of lessons and save parents from giving endless, boring lectures.

The Big Spender

We also let our kids pay with their own money. It is such a grown-up thing for them, and it adds a sense of reality to spending money. When we buy things, we usually pay with cash or write a check. Once in a while we use a debit card. One author recently took a shopping trip with her daughter. Her daughter asked when she could get her own picture card. Her mom assumed she was asking about a driver's license, so she began to explain the driver's license process to her.

When the explanation was finished the little girl scrunched up her nose, put her hands on her hips and said "Mommy, I don't want one of those cards. I want the card that lets me buy things. How can I get one of those?" Her mom told her that when she was old enough, she could get a job and earn her own money. She explained that she could put her money in the bank in something called a checking account. Then the bank would give her a special card that she could use to take money out of the bank to spend at different stores.

After this explanation, she was not at all impressed. "Mommy," she said, "I don't want to work. I just want to buy toys and dresses and stuff." Her mom attempted to explain to her that it doesn't work that way. She told her that we have to earn the money we spend.

How do you get a bull to quit charging?
Take away his credit card.

She obviously didn't understand, but it did lay a good foundation for future conversations. Since then, she has asked many questions about how people get paid and how they pay for things. As you go through your day-to-day life, you will find many creative opportunities to teach financial concepts to your kids, too.

A few weeks after the credit card conversation, the children were sitting around trying to decide what they want to be when they grow up. The middle daughter, the big spender, announced that she wanted to be a "payer and a drawer." It took awhile to figure out what she meant. After some questions and answers, her mom discovered she had found a way around her credit card/no work dilemma. She had heard her parents discussing her grandpa's job. He works as a purchasing agent. She decided that if he can get paid for buying parts and supplies for his company, she should be able to make money buying dolls and clothes. Therefore, she wants to be a buyer. Since, once again, her mom could not seem to help her understand that she could not keep everything she bought as a professional payer (or purchasing agent), she quickly gave up and went on to her other desired profession.

She also wants to be a "drawer." This comes as no surprise, because every morning when she wakes up she heads for her mom's desk, where she has a supply of paper, pencils and pens for her use. She pulls them out and proceeds to make cards and "draw" stories for her friends. She doesn't write stories; she draws them. She draws about the tooth fairy's recent visit, helping her aunt move and taking a trip to Grandma and Papa's. She loves to give these stories and cards to friends and family. We have no doubt that she will someday be a happy little artist, who will hopefully make enough money to buy dolls and clothes to her heart's content.

Draw Interest

Another talented young artist is Mary Catherine Lindsay. She has always had an interest in drawing and decided to incorporate her love for art with her father's business plans and develop a "pretend business" for a school project. She knew she was on to something when she took orders for over $800 worth of stationery on the day she premiered her business, Grasshopper Press.

Her stationery is a combination of either printed or hand-painted designs in bright colors. Mary Catherine first creates her sketch in pencil then goes over the final design in pen. She then paints the various designs of flowers, tents, cars or animals in watercolor. (More information is available at **www.grasshopperpress.com.**)

What began for her as a school project has now turned into a full-service stationery company providing customized notecards, calling cards, announcements and invitations. With the help of her father, Mary Catherine's stationery is currently sold through more than 120 wholesale clients nationwide. This is the perfect example of producing an innovative result by combining a little parental encouragement with a lot of interest from a child.

Children have so many different interests. When kids find something they especially love to do, it is a prime opportunity for parents to encourage them to develop that skill or interest. It may be as simple as providing the tools necessary to pursue their interests (like pencils and paper). Or they may need your help writing a business plan for a school project. Either way, if you pay attention, we think you will be surprised how many ways you can find to teach your children while encouraging them to have fun and learn new things.

What do you get from a nervous cow?
A milk shake.

Cowsistency

One of the most difficult challenges for parents is being consistent. Starting a project, creating guidelines and explaining simple concepts is easy. Consistency is where the rubber meets the road. Most parents face circumstances daily that distract them from being consistent. We are often exhausted, overwhelmed and a little undisciplined ourselves. Yet this is where one of the greatest teaching opportunities comes into play. If you show your kids by example how you set limits, work hard, use your time wisely and take care of what you have, they will be much more likely to mimic those habits. If you can show them that you do not get everything you want when you want it, they will begin to grasp that concept themselves. If you can temporarily ignore the desire to tune out and instead consistently pay attention to your kids and what they are learning from you, you will see amazing long-term and short-term results.

Teach your kids by;

✔ **being an example with your actions,**

✔ **setting limits,**

✔ **working hard,**

✔ **being efficient with your time and**

✔ **teaching them to take care of what they have.**

A friend and her husband discovered a way for their eight-year-old son to make money outside the traditional kid job market. He started by recycling aluminum cans. He collected cans from their home and his dad's office. Once a month he smashed the cans and packed them up to take to the recycling center.

The money he collected from recycling was for a special purpose, not just for buying "stuff." His parents are teaching him to buy assets, not liabilities. If their son had spent his money on "stuff," he would not meet that objective. Instead, he thought of something he could buy (an asset) that would generate even more money.

These parents had thrown around a few ideas with their son, and he'd finally decided to save his money to purchase a bubble gum vending machine. This would lay the foundation for teaching him some basic business principles. It would also introduce him to the concept of passive income and hopefully pique his interest to continually reinvest his profits. He could have firsthand experience of how passive income means that his investment will continue to bring in money for him, yet it will not be dependent on his being involved on an hourly basis. That is the benefit his parents see in this type of kid-friendly business. The benefit for him?

Ultimately, he plans to use the quarters he makes to buy even more bubble gum to sell so that he can then buy the biggest Lego set ever.

The main reasons he was attracted to having a vending machine business are simple. First, he wanted to use some of his left-over money (profit) to buy the huge Lego set. Second, and most important to him, he would be making money doing something he considers "really cool." You see, this boy loves bouncy-ball and bubble gum machines. The first mention of owning one was all he needed to inspire him to smash a few cans. After he had been saving for a while, he was anxious to earn money faster. He expanded his can collection market to include grandparents and other family. He also asked his parents to help him make a flier to hand out in the neighborhood so that he could collect any cans (under parental supervision) his neighbors did not want.

What do little cows get when they do all their chores?
MOOney.

Eventually he saved enough can money to buy a vending machine. He and his parents had initially been looking at a pretty snazzy machine with all of the bells and whistles. When he realized that it would take him four years to save up for this machine, he decided to pursue a less glamorous option. Therefore, his first vending machine was pretty basic.

His parents helped him locate a store that would allow him to place the machine at their entrance. He pays the owner of the store a portion of his earnings from the machine. The remainder he takes home. Of the portion he takes, a certain amount must go to pay for new inventory (bubble gum) to restock his machine when it is empty. He must also put money aside for taxes. (Tax laws vary, so if your child goes into business, consult an expert in the field with any questions.) Another portion of his money goes into a savings fund to buy a larger machine. The remainder he gets to keep for himself.

As this boy began to earn more, his parents set up a few money-handling guidelines for him. His family also uses a job jar to help their kids earn money. When he finishes a project from the job jar, that money is his to spend as he wants. The other money he earns is to be spent differently.

As we mentioned in the previous chapter, a good guide for kids is to divide their money into three categories:

1. Saving
2. Spending
3. Giving

Saving Is a Discipline

The concept of saving is important for kids to learn at a young age. Many adults are late savings bloomers and know firsthand how hard it is to change old habits once they are established for thirty or forty years. There are many great habits kids can learn at a young age. The habit of consistently saving is one of them.

We discussed piggy banks as a useful savings tool in the previous chapter. Depending on how much your children have saved, when the amount becomes substantial, it is a good idea to regularly move piggy bank savings into a special checking or savings account. Many banks offer inexpensive or free savings accounts to young savers.

Spending With Rules

It comes as no surprise to discover that kids find it easy to spend. Their spending money (as opposed to their saving and giving money) is their discretionary fund, and they can do whatever they want with it. Encouraging them to use some of this for short-term savings, as well as spending some immediately, will reap lasting results. Yet it is their money. They will learn a lot from your example and their own experience if you don't control them in this area, but instead guide them. Respect them as the smart little people they are and give them some independence within healthy limits.

Generosity

The third category is for giving. Generosity is a quality that encompasses so much more than finances, and teaching children generosity through finances will influence them in many other areas of life.

The following is a list of tips for helping kids express both financial and non-monetary generosity:

- ✔ Buying canned food to take to a local rescue mission or homeless shelter
- ✔ Donating money to the Salvation Army (their donation boxes are located outside many stores)
- ✔ Donating toys (in good condition) to local charities or children's hospitals
- ✔ Giving money at their Sunday school or church
- ✔ Sharing a special toy with a friend
- ✔ Helping a parent do yard work for a family friend in need

Building a child's financial skills is one way to build greater confidence. Helping kids learn to successfully save, spend and give will not only provide them with a strong financial foundation, but will give them confidence in other areas, as well.

You can communicate to them that you think they are smart, capable and trustworthy. As you learn to remain consistent, despite your successes and failures, you will also gain new confidence as a parent and as the primary role model in their lives.

1. Prevent or treat toy-i-tus. Do not allow your kids to have everything they want, whenever they want it. Help them learn to wait for things they really want. A good rule of thumb is never to buy an item on impulse. Let them (and you) think about it and consider purchasing it on your second visit to that store. This is a great rule for adults also.

2. Two-for-One Rule: When your kids get a new toy, have them give two of their old toys away. We talk about this idea more in Chapter 9, "Giving."

3. Teach children to value what they do have. Set up opportunities for them to earn a little bit of spending money. Let them use some of that money to save up for a special toy.

4. Explain how the ATM works. Discuss how the money got there and that there is not a printing press inside the machine. (Side note: We saw a bumper sticker that said "My Kids Think I'm An ATM." The mother was proudly driving this van around, announcing to everyone that she is okay with her kids thinking they can have money whenever they want. Whose fault is that?)

5. Pick a long-term spending goal with your child. Let them think of a big, reasonable item they would like to earn money to buy, maybe something that is an asset to generate even more money for them.

6. Play store with fun items and real money. Let your kids' practice counting money to pay for things. Start working on counting back change. (So many adults can't count back simple change. This is a valuable skill!)

chapter 5

Fourth to Sixth Grade
"Steer Clear"

• •

There are five coins in all. The total value of the coins is fifty-one cents. Four of the coins are silver. Three coins have ridged edges. One coin has Monticello on its back. What are the coins?

Answer: 1 penny, 1 nickel, 2 dimes, and 1 quarter.

Source: Money Activities That Work

You will never guess where we taught our kids some very important financial lessons. It was in one of the last places you would expect: Disneyland Park. Before you close this book and decide that we are either delusional or profiting greatly from the mention of the Magic Kingdom, think again. We actually found a way to teach our children creative, pain-free lessons about money in an unexpected place. You can do the same by applying the same principles in an amusement park or other attraction near you.

When we take our kids on a vacation to Disneyland Park, we usually give them a limited amount of money (which they can supplement with some of their own) to buy a special toy at the end of the trip. We choose the end of the day to make the purchases for two reasons.

Anticipation

First, waiting until the end of the day teaches them amazing patience and restraint. Every store, booth and sign inspires them to want to spend, spend, spend. Then, when another kid walks by with that cool hat, T-shirt or toy they want, this need for stuff reaches its peak. However, an amazing thing begins to occur by the conclusion of the day; reason begins to overtake them.

Target Shopping

This is when our second purpose for waiting comes into play. After a long day of fun, every toy they see does not have such a magic allure. They have begun to realize that they do not want to spend all of their time looking at toys. By the end of a day at Disneyland, even the most energetic of our children is exhausted and ready to be a target shopper. Only the best toy will do. We then give them a limited amount of time to choose the coolest thing they can find. Therefore, with a little parental encouragement, they get busy and focus on the task at hand.

Realistically, there is a third reason we let them choose the toys at the end of the day. If they wait to buy all of their goodies at the end of the day, we do not have to carry them around all day throughout every ride and attraction! To be honest, this is why we originally started this practice. No, we did not begin with noble intentions. We simply did not want to carry Mickey Mouse around to every ride in the park. Like many things in life, what began for practical purposes turned into an opportunity for all of us to re-learn an even better lesson:

> ## "Good things come to those who wait."
> —Anonymoous

Game Plan

This leads us to another important yet pain-free lesson. It is one you can use to teach your kids a foundational principle for good financial decision making. At the beginning of each trip, decide together which rides you want to go on. Develop a general plan for when you will get there.

Older kids can write down the plan for the family, but be prepared for them to push their agenda for the best rides. Younger ones generally want to go on what the older kids consider baby rides, so if you have kids of varying ages, the compromise begins. It is a great time to work together as a family and act as a team.

In one author's family, their oldest son traditionally declares himself the one in charge of keeping them on schedule. Their middle child makes sure that their oldest is following the schedule correctly. The youngest has the most fun (because she doesn't have a care in the world).

Then they implement something that is absolute genius on the part of Disneyland. When they first arrive, they go to the ride we think will have the longest lines of the day. While there, they obtain a ticket called a FASTPASS. (FASTPASS is not available on all attractions.) They receive a FASTPASS by inserting their Disneyland ticket into a machine near the attraction. They retain their original ticket and the machine gives them another ticket informing them of the time, later in the day, that they may return and get in the FASTPASS line, which usually puts them in line for only five to fifteen minutes, as compared to the usual hour-long wait. With a little planning, they can use FASTPASS for all the most popular attractions and visit the less crowded ones in between.

This concept was not a hard one to get their children to try. After waiting in one- to two-hour lines a couple of times, they all were willing to try anything to avoid that, especially on hot days. Now with a little advance planning, and the willingness to put off going to the ride they want immediately upon entering the park, they happily walk past all of those other poor folks who look tired, frustrated and a little ticked at them for slowing down their fun.

You may wonder why you just received a lecture on the benefits of FASTPASS use. It's to illustrate a fun way that one family showed their children the benefits of delayed gratification and having a plan. A plan allowed them to get much more bang for their buck (or rides in their day). It also gave everyone the chance to go on the rides they wanted. This established at least the beginnings of learning to compromise and work as a team. Waiting to get in line for a ride, although delaying the fun for the moment, allowed them to go on the ride later when the wait was much shorter. This process has not only made their trips more efficient, but much more enjoyable.

Some simple ways to help your children learn the benefits of a plan:

- ✔ Keep a calendar for their use only. Let them write some events on it that are significant to them.

- ✔ Have a special day that the kids plan for the family. They can decide what to serve for meals, when to go to the park and what game the family will play after dinner.

- ✔ Let your child plan a grocery shopping trip. Explain what meals you want to serve, how much money you will spend, and then let him or her (with help for the younger ones) prepare the grocery list.

- ✔ Let each child plan a meal for a family camping trip.

- ✔ As mentioned earlier, let the kids plan together which rides they will go on at an amusement park.

- ✔ Let kids help prepare and price items for a garage sale. They can even help plan where different items for sale will be located.

Children at this age have so much creativity and energy. Allowing them to be involved in making family decisions and plans will show them that you respect them and want their input.

Why did the cow jump over the moon?
To get to the Milky Way!

What is a cow's favorite party game?
MOO-sical chairs.

Why did the farmer feed his cows money?
He wanted rich milk.

Grass Roots Entrepreneur

When Aaron J. Yager was ten years old, he had a life-changing visit with his grandfather: A. J. wandered back into his grandfather's study, and his world changed forever. Bookshelves covered the wall from floor to ceiling. A. J. began quizzing his grandfather about what all these different books were about. His grandfather put down what he was doing and began to discuss with him how these books made him smart and gave him wisdom for success in life.

About a week later, A. J. found a catalog, which showed a stereo system that he wanted very badly. He knew that if he asked his mom and dad for it, they would put him to work in the garden or yard. A. J. knew that there would be a lot of manual labor involved in earning his money from his parents, so he decided to try and find another option.

He went to his grandfather and asked if there was a way he could help him buy the stereo. When he showed him what he wanted, his grandfather offered to make him a deal. If A. J. would work with his grandfather on some projects, he would buy him a stereo that was even better than the one A. J. had found in the catalog. This offer definitely got A. J.'s attention. His grandfather said that if A. J. spent thirty to forty-five minutes a day studying the different books, audio tapes and videos that he gave him

Field Trip Idea:

Factory or Franchise

The more business exposure your family can have the better. If you have any type of factory, manufacturing plant or restaurant franchise in your community, see if you can take a tour. Learn about the operation and the types of products they produce. Determine who the end user is. Identify the many different types of businesses that provide a service or product to this business. Some questions to think about:

- **How many workers do they have?**

- **How secure are these workers' jobs?**

- **Are they seasonal jobs?**

- **What type of skill do they need to work there?**

- **How long have the owners had this business, and what is their background?**

- **For a franchise such as a sandwich shop, find out what caused the owner to buy the business.**

- **What type of hours does it take to run such an operation? What are the good or bad points about local ownership, a franchise, etc.?**

and wrote a paragraph about what he learned each day, he would buy him the stereo.

A. J. immediately agreed. His grandfather said he needed to keep doing this for an entire year, then he could have the stereo. A. J. actually didn't mind because he really wanted that stereo. He accepted the offer, and under the guidance of his parents and grandfather his success program was launched.

That was the beginning of a habit that changed A. J.'s life forever. For the next nine years he spent thirty to forty-five minutes each day reading about, listening to or watching successful people discuss success principles, strategies, tactics and formulas for career and life planning.

This led him, at the age of nineteen, to create the foundation of LifeForce Enterprises, Inc., a company committed to challenging young people to "crank up the volume of their life" and to live and compete successfully in today's world. He also founded a successful web design studio, internet marketing business, entertainment business and publishing company.

A. J. is a great example of a young man who developed the ability to make decisions and learn new things with discipline and fortitude, which carried over to financial matters.

There are many ways we can inspire kids to learn new things. A. J.'s grandfather used his grandson's passion for stereo equipment to "inspire" him to learn new things and stretch himself, thereby earning himself a stereo system in a very unusual way.

To continue in the entrepreneurial spirit, A. J. and his grandfather just started a new company called Smart™ Grandparenting. They are using their success story as the foundation to inspire other grandparents to steer their grandchildren in positive directions. A. J. and his grandfather have collaborated on about thirty plus educational tapes, books and videos to give grandparents the ability to successfully mentor. Their success program empowers both the grandparent as well as the grandchild and covers a myriad of topics. More information on this mentorship program is available at **www.smartgrandparenting.com.**

A. J.'s grandfather had and still has today a significant impact on his life. He implemented several simple, key concepts that any parent and/or grandparent can teach children.

Spend the time to really get to know your child. Do you truly know the answers to the following questions?

✔ How does my child learn best?

✔ What inspires my child?

✔ What are my child's interests?

We all get so busy just dealing with everyday tasks that we often forget to look deeper into our kids' hearts. Take the time to find out more about your children and understand what makes them tick.

"Life is not the destination, it is the journey. So you had better enjoy the trip."

—Anonymous

Earning Moo . . . lah

While not all of us will buy a stereo to provide an incentive for our kids to complete a project, the idea is worth considering. What are some foundational concepts that we want our children to learn or study? How can we creatively inspire them to do so without looking over their shoulder to enforce the learning?

Some of the ways kids this age can earn money:

✔ Help a grandparent with yard work.

✔ Offer to sort through a friend's or family member's CD collection and make sure they are all in the correct case. (This can also be useful for tapes, DVDs and videos.)

✔ Water neighbors' plants, bring in the mail and newspaper and feed the pets when they are on vacation.

✔ Be a partial babysitter at a T-ball game. (A family friend who is in fourth grade loves to sit and play with our three-year-old while we watch the game. All of the parents are right there to help and keep an eye on everyone, but it is easier to pay attention to the older child playing T-ball when we know that our three-year-old is happily playing tag or duck-duck-goose.)

✔ Instead of a car wash, have a bicycle wash for all of the neighborhood kids.

✔ Polish silver for family and neighbors. Most silver needs polishing at least several times per year. Set up a regular cleaning schedule with customers.

✔ Bake and sell goodies to those busy families who don't have time to spend in the kitchen.

✔ Find a way to reward your kids each time they read a book on a specific topic. (Hint: Reward them after they finish the book and summarize it for you.)

A. J.'s grandfather found a way to inspire his grandson to pursue learning in a way that was very appealing. He made the most of an opportunity and used it to lay a foundation for learning that A. J. has carried throughout his life. It was a unique plan, yet it transformed an ordinary young man into an extraordinary young businessman.

Everyone Has Genius

Like A. J., everyone has a natural genius or talent that is unique to them. This means each individual has a unique genetic and personality make-up. At this writing, the newest book on this subject is *A Mind at a Time (Simon & Schuster, 2002)*, written by Mel Levine, M.D. **(www.allkindsofminds.com)**. Dr. Levine shows how parents can identify strengths and weaknesses to determine individual learning styles. By taking the time to understand better how your children learn, you'll know better how to help them grow in their strengths.

Another resource is the Kolbe Index **(www.kolbe.com)**, which is an instrument that measures natural abilities by identifying specific qualities of personal, instinctive strengths. In addition, the Kolbe Index can give you a financial program that coincides with your natural ability. The instrument can identify ways you can reduce financial stress, how you deal best with debt, how you balance risk, how you leverage your talents, how you best make wise decisions, how you deal with change and an overview of your strong points.

There are a number of other instruments available in this area, some online:

✔ www.emode.com

✔ www.davideck.com

✔ www.vitalknowledge.com

✔ www.2h.com

✔ www.personalansir.com

CashCow Kid Out Standing in the Field

Christopher Haas was nine years old when he used his athletic talent (or genius) to develop an invention for a school project. Chris's passion in life was playing basketball, and he was a great shooter. He noticed a lot of his friends and other kids had difficulty shooting baskets because they held the ball incorrectly. So this entrepreneur went home to his garage, dipped his hands into some poster paint and placed them in the correct position on a basketball. Presto! A basketball that shows you exactly where your hands need to be to shoot well. Before long, his school project, as well as a new successful business venture, were underway.

Chris's teachers really liked his idea and encouraged him to promote the project into what is known as the Hands-On Basketball, which has sold more than one million units worldwide. The Hands-On Basketball is a great teaching tool for kids learning basketball basics. The ball is sold in junior and intermediate sizes and has yellow and orange stripes to help show the proper rotation of the ball if it is shot correctly.

Chris, now seventeen, didn't have instant success with his idea, however. He was rejected by twelve companies, yet he didn't give up. It took over a year and a half before one company took a chance on his product. Today, specialty stores across the country carry the Hand-On Basketball and now the Hands-On Football, too. In addition, Chris wrote a book describing the steps he went through to start his own business. The book is called *Shooting for Your Dreams* (Hands-On Press, 1999).

Chris's business, known as Haas Enterprises, is a family venture. At eighteen, his brother published the book and runs Hands-On Press. His sister, eleven, helps with promotions. To get more information on Chris Haas and his company, e-mail him at **haasmjbc@iinet.com** or go to **www.youngbiz.com,** where this and other stories about young entrepreneurs can be found.

Through creativity and determination, Chris was able to develop his passion. He saw an opportunity to build a business while helping others, and he went for it! Chris had a goal, he developed a game plan and then he put it into action. Even during times of tough rejection, Chris didn't give up, and his hard work and perseverance paid off.

Inspiration

As the previous stories illustrate, it is possible for parents (and grandparents and teachers) to inspire kids to pursue their dreams. Throughout their lives, your kids will come up with many unique ideas. Although their financial projects may not become instant successes, their ability to pursue their dreams will carry them on to greater successes throughout their lives.

> "To reach any significant goal, you must
> leave your comfort zone."
> —*Hyrum W. Smith*

1. Look for everyday opportunities to allow your child to develop a plan.

2. Without lecturing, show your kids the benefits of delayed gratification in creative ways.

3. Look for realistic ways that your children can be involved in making decisions.

4. Plan a No Spending Day. This means that for an entire day, no one in the family can spend any money. Plan ahead and come up with as many fun activities as you can that don't cost a cent. By the end of the day, your family will have a new understanding of how many things in life involve money—and how many don't.

5. Give your child the opportunity to compare quality, quantity and price for all your household purchases.

6. Allow your child to pick an age-appropriate summer or short-term "business opportunity" to learn some of the basics of running a business.

7. If you have not already done so, start savings accounts for your children. Allow them to track their savings and interest accumulation.

8. Play store and let your kids practice adding and subtracting with real-life money situations. They should be getting good at counting back change.

chapter 6

Junior High School
(Grades Seven to Eight)
"Making Moo ... lah"

• •

Top 20 Completely Useless Inventions We Found at the Mall

20. *Nonstick cellotape*

19. *Solar-powered flashlight*

18. *Black highlighter pen*

17. *Glow-in-the-dark sunglasses*

16. *Inflatable anchor*

15. *Smooth sandpaper*

14. *Waterproof sponge*

13. *Waterproof tea bags*

12. *AC adapter for solar-powered calculators*

11. *Fireproof cigarettes*

10. *Battery-powered battery charger*

9. *Seatbelts for motorbikes*

8. Hand-powered chainsaw

7. Inflatable dartboard

6. Silent alarm clock

5. Fireproof matches

4. Pedal-powered wheelchair

3. Braille driver's manual

2. Double-sided playing cards

1. Ejector seats for helicopters

(Source: www.brainofbrian.com)

Many entrepreneurs have invented great things, founded unique companies and developed incredible concepts. Some inventions are innovative but not very useful. However, even entrepreneurs who are able to develop ideas that are both innovative and useful do not always find the path to success.

One of the common traits among highly successful people is the ability to set a goal *and* achieve it. Many financially successful people clearly designate daily, weekly, monthly, annual and lifetime goals, and most of these individuals are goal-oriented throughout their lives.

While it may not seem practical to ask the average adolescent to look thirty years into the future, pre-teens and teenagers are not too young to begin learning the steps involved in setting and achieving goals. Kids of all ages can learn to be goal-oriented. Their goals can be large or small. Invariably, they will have some dreams that we will consider unusual. Nonetheless, pursuing their "creative" dreams will help them learn the process of goal setting and achievement.

As parents, we must remember to let our kids choose goals that are of interest to them and keep our expectations realistic as they pursue them. Asking the average twelve-year-old to sit still while you lecture him for three hours a day on the joys of compounded interest is pretty unrealistic. On the other hand, expecting the same twelve-year-old to save up for a new CD player is definitely within the realm of possibility.

> ## "The indispensable first step to getting the things that you want out of life is this: Decide what you want."
> —*Ben Stein*

A Sporting Chance

One way to help your kids learn to set and achieve goals is to encourage them to participate in something they enjoy. For example, many kids have learned valuable lessons about attaining goals through playing sports. Yet even here, their goals need to involve their dreams, not yours. Your son's goal might be just to make the team. Your dream may be to see him start every game, make all-state and be chosen as the MVP. In his life, it must be his dreams that become paramount.

Sports programs are ideal because they involve training and building on small successes. A good coach will not expect an athlete to learn everything she needs to be a successful athlete in one practice. A good coach realizes that athletic training is a gradual process that can be both a fun and educational learning experience.

Ask any successful athlete what it takes to become a champion, and the response will undoubtedly include words like *practice, hard work,* and *determination.* A long-term winner doesn't just wake up one day and magically turn into a champion. That type of success takes years of dedication and sacrifice. One great example of a successful athlete who understands what it means to be a true champion is Tiger Woods.

Tiger began playing the game of golf at a young age. As a boy, his parents encouraged him to develop his golf skills. That encouragement, combined with Tiger's hard work and determination, has helped this golfer become the champion he is today.

Despite his incredible success, he still seeks to improve and develop his golf skills. He understands the importance of having a system to further his success. His is not just a physical pursuit but a mental one as well. Therefore, even when it appears he has it made, he keeps pushing himself. He is the player who will practice the longest, after everyone else has left the course. He sticks to a disciplined routine, complete with physical and mental exercises. He always looks for ways to improve and fine-tune his talents.

With his signature determination and focus, Tiger pushes himself forward to ever-greater heights.

Although Tiger has an incredible amount of willpower and drive, that alone does not explain his huge success. Tiger has a program or plan that he follows to continue to develop and improve his skills. Successfully reaching goals takes more than willpower; it takes a plan.

School sports programs are generally set up so that the teacher or coach will be highly involved in establishing the program or plan. He or she will establish a practice routine, run the drills and then schedule games or tournaments to allow the athletes to compete.

Kids can learn a lot from this process. They can see the goal, which usually involves working successfully as individual players and as a team. They can see that they need a plan to achieve that goal. Players can't just show up for games unprepared. They have to practice. They need to develop both their individual skills and their ability to work as a team. Achieving goals involves some level of effort and usually involves interacting with others. However, if the end result is a success, the effort is often worth it.

The Smaller the Better

Once kids learn the steps involved in setting, working toward and achieving goals, they can carry this skill to other areas of life. The ability to set and achieve goals is one of the fundamental concepts that will help kids successfully handle personal finances. Goals give them direction, a finish line they can aspire to. Goals enable them to move ahead toward a destination.

It is crucial to encourage kids at this age to set reasonable goals for themselves. This is the time to help them rack up as many successes as they can. Celebrate them! Let your kids have a solid foundation of being successful financial goal setters and achievers!

Now, let's backtrack to the beginning of the goal setting process. To start the plan, have your child identify a whole bunch of short-term financial goals.

Some ideas for short-term financial goals:

    ✔ **Open a savings account and deposit $40 in it
       each month.**

✔ Use a checking account for all hobby expenses.

✔ Divide earnings according to the three categories in Chapters 3 and 4.

✔ Read one book each month about a young or innovative entrepreneur.

✔ Raise money for a local charity or giving project.

✔ Identify three new ways to earn extra money, and implement one of them.

✔ Save for a tool or piece of athletic equipment that will help improve skills in school, sports, or a hobby.

Once they choose a goal, help your kids pick a date by which they will attain it. Then, have them identify both the potential obstacles to completing their goal as well as the people or organizations that can help them accomplish it. They can then write out a step-by-step plan. Make sure their short-term goals are broken down to their smallest size. Finally, brainstorm with them and help them identify all of the possible benefits they will obtain by achieving their goal.

Their ability to succeed in a relatively short period of time will give them gratification and confidence that they're making headway in accomplishing their goals. All these small goals create the path to their big goal. These small steps will eventually help them develop their road map to a big goal they will choose in the future. Finally, don't forget to have them put their goals in writing and record their successes. This will give them a permanent record of their victories.

As a reminder, the goal implementation process follows:

1. Identify the overall goal (write it down).

2. Set a specific date for reaching each milestone. (Identify rewards for each milestone)

3. List the obstacles to overcome in order to get to each milestone.

4. Identify the people, groups or organizations needed to help achieve each milestone.

5. Lay out a specific *action plan* to succeed at each milestone.

6. List in detail the *benefits* for reaching each milestone and the overall goal.

The Future Is Now

It is never too soon to start thinking about your child's future. When appropriate for your kids, using everyday situations to teach them to plan for the future can greatly help in the long run. That is what Ben Kaplan's motto was when, as a junior in high school, he started thinking about how he was going to pay for college. He said, "I got that sinking feeling in the pit of my stomach. I was flipping through a glossy college catalog with dreams of bold collegiate adventures dancing through my head, when all of a sudden I got to that page that listed the four-year price tag."

What Ben soon discovered was that there were many scholarships available, even for a student attending a public high school in Eugene, Oregon. Ben diligently applied. He gathered several letters of recommendation, wrote some essays, assembled the packages and sent them off. He was thinking it was a pie in the sky hope that he would win any of the scholarships.

After several months, Ben was shocked when he was notified he had won a $2,500 scholarship. Several weeks later he got a phone call telling him he had just won an additional $15,000. He then started applying for more scholarships and kept finding success.

What happened to Ben was that through trial and error he developed a winning formula. He went on to apply for and win more than two dozen scholarships, totaling nearly $90,000 in unrestricted money, which could be used at the school of his choice. He had enough funds to cover the entire cost of his Harvard education. He graduated debt-free in 1999.

The amusing part of Ben's story is that while he was attending Harvard, he became known as the expert on getting scholarship money. He had students, parents and counselors from all over the country who heard about his success calling to get his advice. So Ben developed a comprehensive guidebook that identified key techniques, strategies, tips and tactics for scholarship success. His book *How to Go to College Almost for Free* (HarperCollins, 2002), became a bestseller. Since then, he's written another successful book, *The Scholarship Scouting Report* (HarperCollins, 2002), which provides behind-the-scene profiles of America's best scholarships.

Ben is known internationally as the Scholarship Coach: His website, **www.ScholarshipCoach.com** provides a wealth of free resources and tools, and a wide range of educational and financial products. Ben says, "Rebel against those who say that financial constraints make it impossible for you to attend this or that school. Steer clear of that excessive student debt. Winning scholarships changed my life, and it can for you, too!"

> "The dictionary is the only place success comes before work."
>
> —*Anonymous*

A Herdful of Ideas

It is important for us to be sensitive to our kids' own timing. Every child is different. Not everyone is going to seriously think about their future by the age of thirteen or fourteen. Are there big interests that your child is beginning to gravitate toward? These may not last forever, but within reason, allow your kids to explore them and prepare for a life of learning and trying new things. This is an age when kids may be willing to attempt many new projects, but finishing them is another story. Therefore, this is also a great time to teach kids that if they commit to a project, unless it becomes detrimental for them, they need to learn to complete it.

While junior high kids may be a little old for traditional job jar projects (as identified in Chapter 2), you can modify that system and incorporate the types of jobs you would like them to help out with. It doesn't hurt if they actually like to do some of the jobs you choose: many yard work chores are definitely within their ability, and they can also help with bigger household projects. Just keep in mind the importance of balancing their need for independence with the priority of spending time together as a family. It is important to tell them and show them that they are both needed *and* helpful members of the family.

Creative Money

Is money creative? No, but it is possible for kids this age to make money creatively! Here are just a few ideas. See our more detailed list of money making ideas in Appendix A.

1. **Entering art contests**

2. **Entering writing contests**

3. **Babysitting**

4. **Pet sitting**

5. **Performing magic**

6. **Being a disc jockey**

7. **Arranging and organizing CD or video collections**

8. **Doing yard work (not so creative)**

Growing up, we had a family friend who loved music so much that when he was in junior high he began collecting albums and stereo equipment. When he started playing his music for parties, weddings and other events, this passion of his developed into a great little business. It became a fantastic opportunity for him when he went on to be a D.J. at a local radio station while still a college student. He successfully turned his passion into a money-making venture.

Emphasize to teens the importance of each step in the business world. Every opportunity provides building blocks to help make them stronger people, and each experience has a lesson, good or bad. No matter the outcome, it can be built on for the future.

One of our good friends is a full-time real estate investor. She says that in her career now, she uses all of her past experience as a former tenant, her business skills from her former career, her accounting knowledge from her undergraduate degree, and her real estate appraisal background from extra courses she took. She uses all her experience in every property she looks at and considers purchasing. The point is, don't let your teen disregard any experience. Every opportunity can influence and teach. We never know when we will need to tap knowledge from a particular expertise or experience.

Who Closed the Gate?

What at first looks like a roadblock may actually be a pasture gate waiting to be opened. Olivia Bennett is a child prodigy in visual arts. Her gift was realized at one of the lowest points in her life. Diagnosed with cancer, at age 5 Olivia endured almost three years of intense chemotherapy, including numerous spinal taps. Her only respite from the pain, nausea and vomiting was painting. At one point, a chemo drug caused nerve damage in her hands so severe that she couldn't even hold a paintbrush. After months of special therapy, Olivia could once again grip her brushes, and she has yet to let go.

Today, Olivia is fully cured at just twelve years old. Olivia's career as an artist has taken on superstar proportions as one magnificent painting after another flows from her pallet. Her work is incredible and can be seen in her book, *A Life in Full Bloom*. Read the entire story of how Olivia overcame cancer to discover her gift and see forty of her most beloved paintings. **www.oliviabennett.com**

Stock Answers

Investing in the stock market is only one of many ways to generate income. This is an area to which many school-aged children are being exposed through various online stock games and analysis projects. Appendix D lists a number of online resources for kid-oriented games and information.

> "The only limit to our realization of tomorrow will be our doubts of today."
> —*Franklin Delano Roosevelt*

Field Trip Idea:
Tour a Car Wash

There are different types of car washes, so try to visit several. There are automated washes with lots of machinery and hand washes with lots of people helping to clean the cars. There are also self-serve car washes where the car owners do all the work themselves, from washing to vacuuming, with all the tools they need available for their use.

- How many employees does the car wash have?
- Are the workers seasonal or permanent?
- Does the facility have vacuum machines?
- Think of all the stuff that the vacuums would suck up. Yuck!
- Ask how many cars per day the car wash washes.
- Estimate the profit margin based on these numbers.
- Why would you want or not want to own a car wash?
- Is location an important factor?

Parents can also set up their own practical family investment scenarios. You and your children can track a particular stock on a weekly or monthly basis and pretend to have invested. This will show how stocks increase and decrease in value. Together, research a company and search for its annual financials and other related articles. The point is to learn in depth about the company, giving children a tangible basis for analyzing business opportunities without the risk. It may seem a little vague to them at first, but eventually they will begin to grasp the concept.

Choose a stock that is kid-friendly so that your kids may see products created by their company. They can follow the stock progress while learning about something they consider fun.

However, contrary to the current trend in children's financial education, we caution you not to treat the stock market as the cure-all for financially educating children. Stock market simulation games do not magically increase financial literacy.

At the heart of the stock market boom in 1999, Robert Kiyosaki, author of *Rich Dad, Poor Dad* (Tech Press, 1997), was invited to speak in a school about the importance of teaching young people financial literacy. After his talk, a teacher raised his hand and proudly said, "We do teach financial literacy in our school. We're teaching kids how to pick stocks."

"Do you first teach them to read the annual reports and financial statements?" asked Mr. Kiyosaki.

"No. I just have them read the reports from the market analysts. If the analyst gives the stock a buy recommendation, we buy, and when they recommend a sell, we sell," the teacher replied.

Kiyosaki reports, "Just before the Enron scandal broke, sixteen out of seventeen market analysts were giving Enron a buy recommendation." His advice: "If you are not financially literate, you shouldn't be picking stocks."

Before kids can understand how to read financial statements and annual reports, they will need to know a lot more about financial analysis than the average junior high student. Do your kids even know the difference between an asset and a liability? Do you? Educate yourself as well as your child. We are not writing any of this to be critical or to point fingers. We are trying to get across that when we have children play stock games that do not require them to learn to accurately analyze a stock choice, we may as well take them to Las Vegas.

The definition of gambling is "to play games of chance for money." Isn't this what we are doing when we ask our kids to pick stocks based on a whim? What are we communicating to them about sound financial decision making?

Robert Kiyosaki's rich dad's words come to mind: "If you want to become rich, start out investing a lot of time before you begin investing a lot of money."

While you want to encourage making sound, informed financial decisions, you do not want kids to become obsessed with making perfect financial choices. They will make mistakes, just as you do. You do not want them to see every mistake, however small, as a catastrophic event. Of course, this may be especially difficult for kids at this age. Life can get a little melodramatic. Just minimize the drama enough for them to see their situation clearly. It may sound trite, but mistakes are great tools for learning. Where would Tiger Woods be if he had left the course the first time he missed a shot? He stayed to face his weaknesses and work and learn ways to improve his game.

Don't let kids obsess over their frustration or embarrassment when a mistake is made: We never want our kids to be defined by their mistakes, whether financial or otherwise.

1. Have a few laughs as a family and brainstorm some useless inventions.

2. Help your kids identify some short-term goals.

3. Have them start identifying their true interests.

4. List tasks they like to do around the house or at school.

5. Find some stock market games on the Internet.

6. List creative ways they could make money outside the house.

7. Discuss the recent changes in the stock market and how they seem to be affecting our national economy.

8. Encourage your kids to learn about other kids who have "creatively" made money.

High School
(Grades Nine to Twelve)
"Out Standing in the Field"

· ·

You know your high schooler needs to expand his or her financial intelligence when . . .

✔ He thinks a credit card is something he can buy from Hallmark to send birthday greetings.

✔ She thinks a budget is a car you rent for a family vacation.

✔ He thinks a financial statement is what his parents say to him when he spends too much money on clothes.

✔ She thinks she can't be overdrawn in her checking account because she still has three checks left in her checkbook.

✔ He thinks a (401)k is a pair of blue jeans.

✔ She thinks a withdrawal is the way someone who is from the South speaks.

Preparing for the future comes naturally to some of us, but for most teenagers the thought of long-range planning is overwhelming. Yet, as you've read in previous chapters, a plan can help them get where they want to go, and it's never too early to start learning this critical life skill.

Start by asking your teens what really interests them, and you may be able to create career options and business ideas out of their responses, even the ones that seem a little outlandish. Don't underestimate their value! Some answers that seem ridiculous or humorous may actually have more potential than you'd think.

That is what happened to two high school seniors from Georgia. Jeff Koon and Andy Powell were interested in funny laws—not fishy laws, but laws that make you laugh because they're so stupid. They compiled a collection of the 101 dumbest real federal, state and city laws in America into a book called *You May Not Tie an Alligator to a Fire Hydrant* (Free Press, 2002). For instance, in Illinois no one may hunt bullfrogs with a firearm; in Massachusetts, it is illegal to dye a bunny rabbit; and in Rhode Island, coasting one's car downhill in neutral is illegal.

These young men not only wrote their first book, they have also become a popular stop on the Internet at **www.dumblaws.com.** Their website is visited by hundreds of thousands of browsers every month. They even have network sites called Dumb Bumpers, Dumb Criminal Facts, Dumb Facts and Dumb Warnings. These laws astonish, possibly outrage and definitely amuse everyone who reads them.

Old Thinking Versus New Thinking

While these young men clearly represent the new generation, most of us grew up during a different time. Most parents were raised hearing the following from their own parents or teachers:

- ✔ Go to school.
- ✔ Study hard to get good grades so you can get into a good college.
- ✔ Get good grades in college so you can get a good job when you graduate.
- ✔ Work hard in your job and stay with that company for years so you can build up a good retirement plan.
- ✔ If you do all of this, you will live happily ever after.

Our grandparents told this to our parents, and our parents downloaded it to us. Is this the mentality you are repeating to your kids? If so, you had better stop and think about it. Times have changed. Many in this new era are gathering information and creating new companies faster than our kids can even decide what flavor of ice cream they want.

> "The world is so fast that there are days when the person who says it can't be done is interrupted by the person who is doing it."
>
> —*Anonymous*

We must not disregard the past. We need to remember the past, learn from it, and pass that knowledge on to our kids. Grow together with your kids as you move toward a new way of looking at things. Gone are the days when you worked for one company for your entire life. Gone are the days when you placed your financial future in someone else's hands. Help your kids see that they can learn from your experience and use that knowledge to make better decisions for themselves.

May the Force Be with You

There are many resources available to help teens with the process of making decisions about their future. If your kids can look at this as a journey, then the knowledge they will gather along the way will make each step a little easier. All the small steps together will create their path to success.

Your kids will probably need help in further defining their interests and getting more direction in their lives. A company called LifeForce can do just that. A. J. Yager, its founder, is the young entrepreneur and author we mentioned in Chapter 5.

The mission of LifeForce is to provide teenagers and young adults with information, knowledge, support and opportunities. The program helps youths realize their dreams, achieve balance in their lives, discover who they are, identify goals and create a plan to achieve them. LifeForce holds seminars and has products and online personal achievement communities designed specifically for youths. Coaches are available to get your teens headed in the right direction. The great thing about LifeForce is that all this education takes place in an entertaining environment.

More information on LifeForce is available at **www.entertheforce.com** and **http://entertheforce.com/youth.htm.** We encourage you to take the time to visit the LifeForce website and explore the resources offered. This is a highly effective program for teens as they begin to plan for their future.

Making Moo . . . lah

As your kids start thinking more about what's next for them, they will hopefully begin to make more decisions and exercise more independence. Money can be one of the biggest areas in which they will want more freedom. Teens don't like to ask for money every time they want to go to the mall, to the movies or out for a snack. It is normal for them to want to

---

Field Trip Idea:

Local Real Estate Firm:

Learn about the real estate market. Find out all the types of transactions the firm handles. Look at prices for different types of properties. Research the pros and cons of each type of property.

- **Talk to agents to find out what type of education and experience they have for this business.**
- **Ask them what they like best about the business.**
- **Tour some open houses.**

Apartment Complex:

A visit to an apartment complex is a great learning experience to see how real estate can become passive income.

- **Talk about all the items the owner of the complex would be responsible for.**
- **Estimate gross monthly rents for the complex.**
- **Guesstimate expenses and therefore the net profit the owner might get.**
- **Talk about absentee owners and how responsibility can be turned over to property managers, who in turn take a fee for their services.**

---

earn extra money in one way or another. However, taking on responsibilities in addition to school can be a big commitment.

There are many traditional ways teens can make money. They can get an hourly job and work at the mall or the corner burger joint. These are great opportunities for kids to get their first taste of life as an employee. They provide an environment where kids can learn responsibility, follow through and how to work under the authority of another. Jobs that involve selling or providing a product also provide an opportunity for kids to learn how to interact with a prospective client.

About fifteen years ago, Burger King had a popular commercial that proclaimed, "Have it your way at Burger King!" That statement was only

Field Trip Idea:

New Residential Subdivision:

Go to the construction site of a new subdivision.

- **Talk about the many facets of the companies involved in the process. These might include engineers, surveyors, graders, plumbers, framers, concrete people, sheetrockers, electricians, roofers, contractors, landscapers, and the list goes on.**

- **Discuss the role of these businesses as subcontractors working under a general contractor, each getting paid for their aspect of the project.**

- **Discuss the skills needed for each facet and how the workers get their training.**

- **Explain the concept behind owning each of these companies and how the owner makes the money and then pays each worker.**

- **How long did the developer of the subdivision own the land before starting the building process?**

- **Understand the process of land speculation and the signs of growth for an area.**

partially true. If you were the customer, you could have it your way. Employees rarely had it their way. People who worked at Burger King learned a specific system designed to ensure that customers always got what they wanted; employees got to do what the *customer* wanted.

It may not always seem "fair" to a working teen that the customer's needs come first. Yet exposing your kids to this environment can show them what life can be like in the real business world.

If your kids don't want to take the traditional route, consider helping them start their own businesses. There are an endless number of money-making ideas for teens worth exploring. (To assist you in this process, CashCow Kids™ has a supplemental workbook that walks kids through the process of starting and building their own businesses. It is available on our website, **www.cashcowkids.com.**)

Slam Dunk Opportunity

A great example of shooting big is the summer business started by the O'Connell brothers. For the past five years, Sean, age nineteen, Brendan, age eighteen, and Paddy, age sixteen, have run a summer basketball camp in River Forest, Illinois. The interesting thing about the O'Connell brothers is that none of them played organized basketball after grade school. However, they do excel in other sports. But, because the boys play basketball all the time at home, they realized they could teach grade-school kids basic basketball skills, such as dribbling, passing, shooting and rebounding.

The brothers decided the basketball camp would be the perfect fit for them, especially with their aversion to yard work and other physical labor. Because the start-up costs were low and they already had a hoop and several balls, they were willing to give it a go. The brothers knew a lot of kids in their neighborhood. Therefore, just by handing out fliers in the area, their first camp session involved twenty boys and girls. The kids came to the camp for two hours a day for two weeks.

The O'Connells have steadily grown their business to fifty kids and have expanded it to two two-week sessions. The business has shown a profit every summer, even after paying for expenses such as t-shirts, snacks and prizes. Because of the boys' business savvy and their ability

ability to work with kids from five to twelve years old, the business has been a success.

Each of the brothers has defined responsibilities. Sean runs the daily camp activities. During the first hour, the campers learn basketball fundamentals. After snack time, they spend the second hour playing various games and practicing new skills. Brendan handles the record keeping, which includes tracking each camper's progress during the camp. Paddy, the youngest brother, makes sure everyone gets their snack, treats any injuries and schedules bathroom breaks.

Now five years into the business, some changes are occurring. This year, when the garage was remodeled, the family basketball hoop was torn down, so the camp will move to a nearby community center. This change will add extra expenses and travel time for everyone. Brendan and Paddy will also take on new responsibilities because Sean will be staying at college this summer. However, they found a willing assistant who has been attending the camp since it first began.

The brothers have a great time running this business. It is fun for them to teach sportsmanship and encourage their campers' skills as they improve. More information on the O'Connell's camp is available on **www.youngbiz.com,** where this and other stories about young entrepreneurs can be found.

"We all find the time to do what we really want to do."
—William Feather

Where Do You Get Your Income?

Help your kids do their research before jumping into something that takes on a life of its own. The O'Connells' situation is a great seasonal business that doesn't interfere with the busy school year. They are a great example of how work doesn't necessarily mean going out and finding a job and collecting a paycheck. Work doesn't have to be just going through the motions. It can come in many different forms, essentially from three general categories.

In the first category, they can earn money working for someone by completing a task as a consultant or an employee. They will work and then get paid. The income they earn from this category is the most highly taxed type of income and the category most people's incomes fall into.

The second type of income is passive. This generally includes businesses that a person owns but doesn't actively participate in as well as investments such as real estate. This income is called passive because it is earned as a result of the investment. A person may manage various aspects of the real estate or oversee some issues of the business. Yet by and large, one doesn't need to put in a traditional work week to earn this income. That is why it is called passive: It is not a direct result of "active work." As well as the lack of time constraints, another big plus to receiving income from passive opportunities is the tax benefits.

The last category of income comes from paper assets. These assets include a variety of investments that would be included in a portfolio of stocks, bonds, mutual funds, etc. This category can be taxed as high as the earned income category or have many of the numerous advantages of passive income. It all depends on how the accounts are structured. Consult with the appropriate professionals to maximize the tax advantages for each situation.

Your kids may want to pursue earning income from one specific category, or they may want to try their hand at a few different types of money-making opportunities. Whatever venue they decide to pursue, it is important to help your kids develop a financial plan. Once they begin to make money, they need to have a plan to get their money working for them. Even at this age, help them create a plan to invest their money so it's working for them and they're not working for it.

Millions Makin' Bacon

One young lady who invented her own opportunity to create residual income is Abbey Fleck. Abbey was eight years old when she saw her dad cooking bacon in the microwave one Saturday morning. Because they were out of paper towels to soak up the grease after removing the bacon from the microwave, the fat was just dripping off the meat. Abbey said to her dad, "It's too bad we can't just cook the bacon while it was hanging."

This was the moment her million-dollar idea was created.

They both thought it was a brilliant idea, that same day Abbey and her dad got busy and started making some prototype models. They inserted wooden dowels and pieces of plastic coat hangers into a glass dish, loaded it with bacon, and put it in the microwave. It worked! The fat dripped off the bacon. After refining their prototype with better materials, the Makin Bacon® dish came into being.

The Flecks knew the Makin Bacon dish was a product with strong potential, so they initially offered it to big retailers. They were turned down. They then went to the Armor Company, makers of Armor brand bacon. Armor liked the idea and placed an ad for the Makin Bacon dish on the back of each Armor Bacon package. To receive the dish in the mail, customers sent $6.99 and a UPC barcode symbol from the bacon package.

Abbey's invention gained popularity by word of mouth, and she became a company spokesperson. Over the last six years Abbey, now fifteen, has appeared on *Oprah, Dateline NBC, 20/20,* and *The Late Show with David Letterman.* She has also been interviewed by numerous newspapers, magazines and radio shows.

All the press coverage got the attention of the big retailers whom they had initially approached. Eventually they received a distribution agreement with a national chain store (Wal-Mart). At this point, the Flecks were short on the cash needed to create the hundred thousand dishes required per their agreement with Wal-Mart. Abbey's grandfather, George Fleck, took out a loan on his farm so Abbey and her dad could have the capital they needed to launch their company into the big leagues.

Abbey is now co-owner, along with her dad, of A de F, Inc., which sells approximately 624,000 Makin Bacon dishes a year. These huge sales bring the Flecks royalties of over one million dollars a year. This is a great example of passive income generated from an opportunity one young entrepreneur found and filled. More information on Abbey Fleck is available at **www.makinbacon.com** and **www.youngbiz.com.**

Create Assets

The old saying, "the rich get richer and the poor get poorer" is true in many ways because the rich build businesses, create new assets and limit their liabilities. The poor and middle class do what previous generations did. They work harder and harder for earned income, the highest taxed income. In addition, most middle-class families get themselves deeper into debt just trying to survive.

As we have illustrated with the multitude of success stories in this book and on our website, teens can excel in many arenas. Help your kids get started by encouraging them to explore the areas in which they have talent, strengths and a strong interest. Evaluate their true passions at this point in their life. Their hobbies can be a great place to start. What do they love to do in their spare time? It can't be homework!

> "The greatest good you can do for another is not just to share your riches, but to reveal to him his own."
> —Benjamin Disraeli

If you become a student of the wealthy, you quickly learn that most people who earn more than six figures attribute their financial success directly to truly loving what they do for a living. Keep that in mind as you advise your kids regarding their future. As they pursue different interests, they will discover what they truly like to do and what really makes them happy. Developing those interests will help them arrive much more quickly at success.

Once a business idea hits, help your kids figure out when and how to do it. Spend time with your teen and help them do their homework. Research all aspects of the business. It is better to invest some time up front before you start pouring money into the new venture. Know what you are getting into. Key business concepts and principles are universal and can apply across the board. When necessary, have them talk to professionals and do their research!

We have identified some potential business ideas to get you thinking. Of course, you can come up with more creative ideas yourself. You can also go to our website, **www.cashcowkids.com,** for the most up-to-date information. In addition, Appendix A contains a list of money-making ideas.

Down on the Farm

The Chocolate Farm is a unique business founded by two young entrepreneurs, Elise and Evan Macmillan. These creative kids specialize in making and teaching about chocolates. Elise, now fourteen, began making candy with her grandmother at the ripe old age of three. She continued the art on her own and official production began about three years ago. Evan, age sixteen, directs the financial and information management at the company. He designed and maintains the Chocolate Farm's popular website.

The Chocolate Farm received the Ernst & Young Entrepreneur of the Year Award in 1999 and was rated the top youth food business in the USA in 2001. The company was selected to sell its chocolates during the inaugural season at the Denver Broncos' new football stadium. It has been featured in a variety of publications and has appeared on numerous television shows.

Elise and Evan are also the authors and publishers of *The Chocolate Farm Cookbook* and recently launched their newest product, the "Chocolates By You" Kit. Their complete product line and company information is available on their website, **www.chocolatefarm.com.**

College and Beyond

As the future approaches, the big decision of "where to go from here" will become a critical choice for your kids.

- ✔ **What will they pursue after high school?**
- ✔ **Do they want to go to college?**
- ✔ **What college are they going to attend?**
- ✔ **What will their major be?**
- ✔ **Do they want to get a job?**
- ✔ **What do they want to be when they grow up?**

These are probably just some of the many questions your kids are sick of hearing by now. You and your teens are probably planning for their future. By staying focused on the big picture, your teen can have a broader context from which to choose.

Today, teens face a different job market than past generations, and a good education may be an important key to open the doors of opportunity. A formal college education is not appropriate for everyone, and there are many highly successful entrepreneurs who barely managed to, and some didn't, finish high school. But if your kids have the opportunity and the means to get a higher education, it can serve a great purpose. On the flip side, statistics show that earning levels are not always equivalent with education levels.

Teens who are high-energy self-starters may do well pursuing some type of entrepreneurial program, offered at universities and colleges all over the world. Many of these programs allow students to explore their specific areas of interest and take them to a new level.

In addition, if your kids have or want to start a business while still in high school, finding an entrepreneurial program will allow them some flexibility to keep the business going while furthering their education. It might be a great way to fine-tune business skills.

There are even summer programs and camps specifically for young entrepreneurs. If this is something that interests your kids, help them do some research and start exploring the possibilities. We identify some of these programs on our website.

While allowing them to enjoy their high-school years, try to find creative ways to help your kids expand their financial knowledge. They may embrace the concept of creating a financial plan for their future, or they may gaze at you in horror when you propose such a concept. Either way, help your kids develop a plan that will work for them and help lay the foundation for the greater financial independence they will face during the upcoming college years.

> "If you don't know where you are going, you will probably end up somewhere else."
> —*Laurence J. Peter*

1. Help your teen determine current interests and passions.

2. Help your teen learn as much as possible about money.

3. Encourage your teen to ask a lot of questions.

4. Talk to your teen regularly.

5. Help your teen get her own checking account (if she doesn't already have one).

6. Assist him in opening a savings account (if he doesn't already have one).

7. Encourage your teen to start keeping accurate records (or a-cow-nting).

8. Find and share success stories of young entrepreneurs.

9. Explore the possibility of helping your kids connect with a life coach to guide them in the right direction and keep them on track. You can search the Web for "teen life coach" as a good starting point.

10. Play money games as much as possible: Monopoly is a great place to start, or try Cashflow 101.

11. Talk with your teen about the key components of running a business.

12. Brainstorm regularly and keep an ongoing list of money-making ideas.

13. Promote reading, listening to tapes and attending seminars on money/finance and entrepreneurial ideas.

14. Encourage your teen to talk to your friends, their friends and businesspeople about money/financial issues.

College

"Avoid the Cow Pies"

Dear Mom and Dad,

$chool is going $ooo well. I'm $tudying a lot and $taying on track for final$. $taying busy with the $occer team a$ we are traveling to $pain. $ure do mi$$ you and my $ister. $ee you $oon this $ummer.

Your Loving $on,
Nolen $amuels

Dear NOlen,

Glad to kNOw you are NOt flunking out of school. We are looking forward to your return this summer to our family maNOr in the NOrtheast. We kNOw that the kNOwledge you're getting will be an eNOrmous advantage for you to find a NOtable job this summer.

With Love From Your NOrmal Parents,
Mom and Dad

The New Frontier

Every year, approximately three million teens enter the wide-open territory of "real life" after high school. This new stage of independence will expose them to an entirely new frontier. For most, this will be their first experience in braving life on their own. Their adolescent dreams of freedom and independence will finally come true. Opportunity will knock, and they will run to embrace it!

The Bottom Line

As exciting as this adventure may seem, your kids will soon discover that freedom comes at a price. As they start to plan their escape to this new frontier, they will encounter a few unexpected surprises along the way. Independent people pay their own way. Surprise! Independent people make their own decisions and then live with the consequences. Surprise! Independent people are responsible for themselves and their choices. Surprise!

It is critical that you and your kids have open communication regarding financial matters. Now is the time to help them prepare for the financial challenges and opportunities they are about to face. While it won't prevent every predicament, this preparation will help them successfully handle many obstacles.

You may or may not help your kids cover some of the financial responsibilities they will encounter during this new independent stage in their lives. Whatever you decide, it is important to clearly communicate and differentiate between their responsibilities and your contribution.

Whether they are away at college, training for a vocation or out in the work force, your kids will be learning how to cope with many new issues. Some of the things they will need to balance may include their studies, a new social life, roommates, time and money. Some college students will thrive on this opportunity and handle it extremely well. Others will have a more difficult time, forced to learn by the school of trial and error.

"I have always grown from my problems and challenges, from the things that don't work out, –that's when I've really learned."
—Carol Burnett

While nothing you can do will make this journey completely smooth for them, the following tips will help your young adults avoid some of the financial cowpies they might encounter along the way.

Tip #1: Find a Solid Source of Income

Your kids will be exposed to myriad ways of generating money. Yet if they're attending a college, university or vocational school, their time will be limited. It will be challenging enough for them to balance attending classes, studying and their social lives. Adding work to the mix will increase the challenge significantly. Ideally, your kids have already found a source of income that will allow them to make the most money possible while putting in as little time as necessary. Yet developing such an income-generating opportunity will take research and planning.

> ### Field Trip Idea:
> ## Life ... Enjoy the journey!
> Your field trip for this time of life? Life itself. Remember to enjoy the path along the way and don't be in a rush to get to the end. It is the journey that can bring the most rewards, not just reaching the finish line.

Sources of income for your college kids may include parental contributions, scholarships and grants, jobs, investments . . . the list goes on. Their list of options is enormous. After narrowing the selections, help your kids focus on the best opportunities.

As we discussed earlier, make sure your kids are clear on the scope of their financial game plan. If you have conditions for the money you give them, let them know this up front. Help your kids understand that this is their financial plan, not yours. Convey to them that they are now steering the ship and you will be occupying the role of trusted advisor.

> ## "Achievement is largely the product of steadily raising one's levels of aspiration and expectation."
> —*Jack Nicklaus*

A successful person is often someone who is willing to do what others will not. Many college students do not want to go through the hassle of filling out the paperwork required to apply for grants and scholarships.

Maybe that is why millions of dollars in scholarship money go unclaimed each year. Scholarships and grants are great options for generating money. As we discussed in Chapter 6, one enterprising young man, Ben Kaplan, developed a winning formula for acquiring these funds. He personally collected enough funds to virtually cover the entire cost of his Harvard education. His statement bears repeating: "Rebel against those who say that financial constraints make it impossible for you to attend this or that school. Steer clear of that dreaded student debt. Winning scholarships changed my life, and it can for you, too!"

One of the most common ways young adults choose to generate income is through jobs. Their employment opportunities may range from working at a local restaurant to working as an intern at a law firm. The key will be for them to find an opportunity that will allow them to leverage their limited time to obtain a maximum return. They will also be more inspired to work if they can find a job they thoroughly enjoy!

Ideally, your kids will be able to find investments that will generate as much passive income as possible. The concept of passive income involves working hard initially to build a business and/or investment in return for a constant income stream that will continue for months and/or years with minimal maintenance. Some great ideas for passive income streams are included in the money making list in Appendix A.

It may seem that a busy college student will be unable to find the time to manage a business or develop an income-generating investment. Yet, isn't this the same excuse most of us with normal jobs have used throughout our careers? The following examples show that with a little creative planning, it can be done.

Launderette

Why not own a self-service laundry establishment? This type of business would require daily collection of money from the business, cleaning and maintenance of the machines and regular upkeep and monitoring of the facility. But the beauty of this type of business is that it is not as time intensive as a regular eight-to-five job. It gives you the freedom of flexible hours and the ability to make a reasonable profit, if it's in the right location. Your studying can be done while you sit behind the counter.

Vending Business

Perhaps your kids live in a dorm where there are no vending machines. Encourage them to find out how to buy and place machines on campus and collect the money. Again, the idea is to invest limited time while generating cash flow. The vending machine idea can work in many different venues. Let them use their creativity. Examples could include restaurants, stores, golf courses, educational facilities, office buildings and shopping centers, to name just a few.

Real Estate Investor

We know of several college students who developed successful businesses as real estate entrepreneurs. Getting started was their biggest obstacle, but they were able to overcome that by obtaining as much sound advice as they could from experts in the field. One such resource is Dolf de Roos, Ph.D.

Have you ever heard of a doctor who never had a job? Well, Dr. de Roos is one. He was raised in a family that believed the formula "to do well" was to study hard, earn a degree, get a good job and build a career. When Dolf was a freshman in college, he wanted to know what traits the rich all had in common. After nine months of study, he realized it wasn't age, gender, inheritance or even education.

The two things Dolf found the rich people tended to have in common were:

1. integrity (their word was their honor) and

2. they made or held their wealth in real estate.

Thus, at the young age of seventeen, Dolf decided to start investing in real estate. He was also a perpetual student and spent eight years at a university completing his Ph.D. in electrical engineering. Upon his graduation, Dolf had several interviews and job offers. He received one job offer with a salary of $32,000 per year, which at the time was a large sum of money. Unfortunately for his prospective employer, the week before Dolf received this job offer, he had just closed a real estate deal in which he netted $35,000. He wondered why anyone would want to go work for a firm for forty hours per week, fifty weeks a year and make less than what he made on one real estate deal in one week. As you might imagine, Dolf did not accept that job, and to this day he has never had a job. He owns real estate all over the world and still enjoys looking at and buying properties. Dolf has written a number of books on gaining wealth from real estate, has created software products, holds seminars and provides educational opportunities throughout the world. More information on Dolf's products and events can be found at **www.dolfderoos.com**.

Network Marketing

Network marketing is another business opportunity in which energetic people can sometimes see quick success. A number of multilevel marketing companies sell quality products to consumers. If your kids are serious about this type of business, encourage them to do their research and be realistic in projecting their income. Learning as much as they can in advance, before they jump into this type of business, is key. Initially, it can take a lot of hard work. However, the payoff down the road, as they begin to generate passive income, can be worth all of the advance preparation. If your kids have an abundance of potential client contacts, such as in a dorm setting, they may already have a huge advantage.

Many of these network marketing companies are starting to take note of the potential among sixteen- to twenty-four-year-olds as more than just customers, but also as sales representatives. One example is Avon, the big direct seller of beauty products. In the fall of 2003, Avon will launch a new cosmetics line targeted at the sixteen- to twenty-four-year-old age group. This new line is called "mark." It will have hip packaging and appear more upscale than other teen-focused brands. Avon intends to target young women in high schools, colleges, malls and other places where young people gather. Andrea Jung, Avon's chief executive officer, says, "It is recreating the Avon earnings opportunity." She notes that with a difficult job climate, selling the new mark line may be more desirable for teens and young women. More information about Avon and its products can be found on the company's website, **www.avon.com** and **www.meetmark.com**.

"Our imagination is the only limit to
what we can hope to have in the future."
—*Charles F. Kettering*

Tip #2: Create a Consumption Plan

No matter your income, everyone needs a household Consumption Plan. This is not a budget. The word budget has a negative connotation, especially to college students. In contrast to what they cannot do, help your kids develop a plan that outlines how much they can spend every month. A Consumption Plan will allow them to spend by choice, not on impulse.

It is important that your kids know where their money is going, what their major expenses are and how much money they can save and/or invest each month. They will be amazed at how much money can be spent on little things like lattés, fast food, soda drinks, and other incidentals. These small amounts can really add up. By planning, they can choose where they want to spend their money and where they will not spend it.

Developing a Consumption Plan can actually be fun for them if they focus on the opportunity to choose how they will spend. Encourage them to set milestones along the way. When they reach a pivotal point, help them choose a reward. Their reward doesn't always have to be monetary, but the success should be celebrated.

If your kids are disciplined and can stick to a strict Consumption Plan, they may not need much guidance in this area. However, if they have trouble controlling their spending, help them learn what works to help them stay on track. One idea is to create an Envelope Consumption Book. This involves creating an envelope for each category of spending or saving. At the beginning of each month, they can put the cash allocated for that category in the indicated envelope. This will train them to get into the habit of knowing how much goes where. It will also help drive the point home that when the money is gone, it is gone.

Some general categories you may want to include in a Consumption Plan:

1. **Savings**

2. **Expenses**

3. **Giving**

The first category, savings, is for putting money away for goals and emergencies. Encourage your kids to put some money in this category every month, even if just a small amount. Set this money aside even before the bills are paid each month. This concept is so important that we introduced it back in the preschool and K–3 chapters. This doesn't mean they should take the money and go out and spend it on a new pair of shoes, although at this age, you will not be able to dictate how your kids spend every penny. Your kids will soon discover, on their own, that if they get into the habit of saving part of what they earn, they will have money to achieve their future goals. Even a little stash of cash in their savings account will help them cope better when the pasture isn't green.

> ## "Lack of money is no obstacle. Lack of an idea is an obstacle."
> —*Anonymous*

The second category, expenses, is for paying bills such as rent, utilities, food, and for other items they have identified as necessities. This category within their Consumption Plan will guide them as they decide how much to spend on both the necessities and the little extras.

The third category, giving, is an essential category in any Consumption Plan. We consider this topic so important that we have devoted an entire chapter to it.

The Consumption Plan, including saving, expenses and giving, will keep your kids in check and help them choose to both live below their means and stay on their path to financial freedom. This plan will allow them to choose their standard of living. Then, as earnings increase, they can choose to keep their standard of living nearly the same.

Tip #3: Step Over the Cowpie of Credit

A college history professor asked his class, "What do you think was the greatest invention of all of time?"

One student answered, "The wheel."

Another student offered, "The printing press."

Yet another student answered, "The computer."

Then someone chimed in from the back of the room, "The credit card!"

Unfortunately for many kids in school, a credit card may indeed look like the best thing going. With a tight budget and a culture of consumption, credit can look like salvation. But it's a wolf in cow's clothing. Help your kids watch out for wolves roaming the pasture.

We have seen a lot of our friends carry debt from college, which can continue to grow and snowball for many years afterward. Debt for young adults can come from several sources. However, we have primarily seen it in the form of student loans and credit card debt. Both of these areas, especially credit card debt, can get out of control quickly.

> **In 1999, one large credit card company spent over ten million dollars marketing credit cards to high school and college students.**
>
> **According to a 2000 survey conducted by Sallie Mae (a major resource for student loans), the average credit card balance of a college student is $2,748 and nearly ten percent of students owe creditors more than $7,000.**

Merchants and credit card companies alike teach us that spending is fun, exciting and exhilarating. This may be true, but the flip side can be devastating. What many young people don't realize is that what can take days to spend can take years—even decades—to pay off. If they aren't careful, their debt will be dictating their future.

The first credit card was issued by American Express in 1951.

Young adults are not the only prey. All the advertising messages attempt to make credit-based spending irresistible. Yet if your kids can learn to resist the marketing campaigns now, they may be able to carry this financial savvy with them throughout the rest of their lives.

Credit card debt for college students is one of the messiest cowpies out there. Of course, it is a huge problem for all ages, but it seems that college-age teens/young adults are particularly likely to "step in it."

> ✔ **A recent credit-card tracking study reported that last year, Americans charged more than four hundred billion dollars on their credit cards. The interest paid: a shocking fifty billion dollars.**

✔ There are over one billion cards in circulation now, with an average balance of $5,800 and an interest rate of 18.3 percent.

✔ The average American has eight to ten credit cards.

If your kids currently have credit cards, encourage them not to carry a balance on them from month to month. If they do have a balance, challenge them to make paying it off a priority. They can transfer their balance to a card offering a super low introductory interest rate to help pay the balance off more quickly. Just remind them not to use their first card as well as the second or they will compound their difficult situation.

If your kids like to use credit cards for convenience, encourage them to establish a debit card where they can deposit money into an account and access it with the use of plastic. This will allow them the convenience of a credit card, while keeping their spending under control and avoiding high monthly interest rates.

The best credit plan is to put one hundred percent down and have no monthly payments. Encourage your kids to be conscious about using money efficiently. They don't have to be a miser or a penny pincher. They just need to decide to use their common sense when making financial choices.

Tip #4: Have a Wealth Plan

Help your kids identify their future goals now. The sooner they plan for the future, the stronger their financial picture will look. Let them identify where they want to be financially in five years, ten years, and so on. Then help them identify a game plan to get them there. This game plan will develop into their Wealth Plan.

Whether your kids are full-time students, spending most of their time studying and working part-time; part-time students with a life full of study and work; or working full-time, they will need to plan for their future. Regardless of where they are in their lives, their future is up to them. If they aren't achieving their goals, they will end up helping someone else achieve theirs.

"When you don't know what you want, you often end up where you don't want to be."
—*Bob Greene*

One college student learned about credit the hard way. Phillip Lechter started receiving "real mail" during his freshman year in college, when he turned eighteen. Prior to that time, he was living at home and the only letters for him were photo radar tickets (a.k.a. speeding tickets) and an invitation to enlist in the Navy.

The first piece of real mail he received was a credit card application promoting a five-hundred-dollar line of credit with payments of only fifteen bucks per month. He thought, "What a deal!" Then he called the toll-free number, and he was five hundred dollars "richer."

He maxed out that card quickly, only to find another letter in his mailbox with an encouraging message that his line of credit had been raised to one thousand dollars. He was really set. All Phil had to pay was thirty dollars per month. He knew he was getting into the so-called rat race. His reality check came when he realized he was a college freshman with $1,250 in credit card debt (including his new department store credit card) with minimum monthly payments of $50—and no job.

So Phillip got a job and worked twenty hours a week for the next four years to pay off that debt. He estimates that including late fees and finance charges he paid over $1,900 to wipe out $1,250 in credit card debt.

The other side of the equation that Phillip didn't fully understand was the impact of thirty-, sixty- or ninety-day late payments on his personal credit rating. He began to realize this when he started working as a leasing professional who rated his clients' credit. It was then that Phillip took a look at his credit rating. Ouch!

It took him months to clear up old and inaccurate information. Now he checks his report every six months and works hard to keep it clean.

No more credit for Phillip. Well, he does take credit for learning at a young age how important it is to protect your credit rating.

(Source: *Rich Dad's Straight Talk Newsletter,* October 2002,
The Learning Curve: "Give Me Some Credit!" by Phillip Lechter)

Help your kids identify their current financial situation.

✔ How do your kids make their money?

✔ Do they have a job?

✔ Do parents or grandparents help them financially?

✔ Do they generate any income from investments?

✔ What can they do to improve their finances?

✔ What do they want their situation to be?

Help them think creatively about how they can build their wealth. How can they maximize their money to work the best for them? Encourage them to explore ways to build businesses and create assets that bring in passive income every month. As they continue to explore new ways to build wealth, new opportunities will pop up every day. They will soon realize that the more wealth builders they find, the more opportunities they will encounter.

A great book that inspires one's potential millionaire qualities is *The One-Minute Millionaire: The Enlightened Way to Wealth* (Harmony Books, 2002) by Mark Victor Hansen and Robert G. Allen. This book is available from their website, **www.oneminutemillionaire.com.**

Multiple Streams

As we mentioned, there are a myriad of options your kids can pursue to help pay their way during their young adult years and beyond. A common attribute among wealthy and successful entrepreneurs is they all have multiple streams of income. This is a great concept for everyone. Diverse sources of income create a greater probability of constant cash flow. Your kids may decide to invest in an existing business, start a new business, invest in real estate, write a book, invent a product or join a network marketing group. Their challenge will be to identify and capitalize on great opportunities when they present themselves.

Tip #5: Develop Strong Mentors

A great way your kids can strengthen their Wealth Plans is to pursue strong mentors. Once your kids have an idea of the direction they want to go, encourage them to look for leaders who have been successful in that same field. You may even have a network of friends they could meet with to begin their quest.

> "Keep away from people who try to belittle your ambitions. Small people always do that, but the really great people make you feel that you, too, can become great."
> —*Mark Twain*

The benefit of shadowing a current leader in their field of interest could be huge in the long run. You can help your kids research these individuals to ensure a good fit for all involved. Encourage them to learn all they can from their mentors, yet retain their ability to analyze each situation and think critically and independently. Help kids discover how the mentor got started, what their goals were and are, how they established their fundamental business practices and any other advice the mentors are willing to share.

Graze the Greener Pastures

Your kids may come up with some unusual money-generating ideas along the way. No idea is dumb, crazy or too simple. Just help them do their research. People like Michael Dell, Bill Gates, Walt Disney and Ray Kroc succeeded because they had one great idea, which they took and developed. It may have taken a few tries, but they succeeded.

Become your kids' biggest supporter by helping them go for their dreams and stick to their goals. Give them sound financial advice so they can find their path to financial freedom and not be held back by financial constraints.

1. Help your kids develop a Consumption Plan and live below their means.

2. Each month, encourage your kids to get in the habit of paying themselves first.

3. Help your kids identify their poor spending practices and try to change them.

4. Help them avoid improper use of credit.

5. Assist them in developing a Wealth Plan with a winning strategy. Their passions will dictate what type of plan they will stick to. (For example, our passion for homes led us to our passion of buying and selling real estate.)

6. Emphasize the importance of multiple streams of income to secure their future.

7. Encourage them to keep an open mind to new opportunities.

8. Help them develop strong mentors.

9. Remind yourself that they are now the captain of their ship. Your role is now one of a trusted advisor.

10. Let your kids know they can succeed in anything, if they put their mind to it.

Giving
"Cream Always Rises to the Top"

• •

There are two seas in Palestine. One is fresh, and fish are in it.
Splashes of green adorn its banks. Trees spread their branches over
it and stretch out their thirsty roots to sip of its healing waters. The
River Jordan makes this sea with sparkling water from the hills. So
it laughs in the sunshine. And men build their houses near to it, and
birds their nests; and every kind of life is happier because it is there.
The River Jordan [also] flows on south in to another sea.
Here is no splash of fish, no fluttering leaf, no song of birds, no
children's laughter. Travelers choose another route, unless on
urgent business. The air hangs heavy above its water,
and neither man nor beast nor fowl will drink.
What makes this mighty difference in these neighbor seas?
Not the River Jordan. It empties the same good water into both.
Not the soil in which they live; not in the country round about.
The other sea is shrewder, hoarding its income jealously. It will not
be tempted into any generous impulse. Every drop it gets, it keeps.
The Sea of Galilee gives and lives. This other sea gives nothing.
It is named the Dead.

There are two kinds of people in this world.
There are two seas in Palestine.

(From The Man Nobody Knows *by Bruce Barton)*

The two seas of Palestine illustrate how our everyday choices can lead us down diverse paths. Think about the others in your pasture. What are they like? Which sea do they resemble? What type of person are you? Do you give and live?

The Joyful Giver

While much of today's financial education focuses on areas ranging from saving to investing, the topic of giving, if addressed at all, is usually a side note. We believe giving is much more important than that. Giving should be a lifestyle habit. In the United States we are blessed with amazing resources, both financial and otherwise. This is both a privilege and a responsibility.

Many prosperous people attribute part of their financial success to their ability to give to others. They are able to see beyond their own personal goals to the needs of others. If one takes the time to study the wealthy, most of them place giving as a high priority.

"Go behind the scenes of most great fortunes,
you'll find a common pattern—
the more they gave, the more they got."
—Mark Victor Hansen and Robert G. Allen

While it may seem that only the rich can give any kind of substantial contribution, this is not the case. We have seen generosity come from the most unexpected places. Often those who seem to have little to give financially show themselves to be incredibly generous. Their generosity does not always involve money. Yet their cheerful attitude in sharing what they do have leaves a lasting impression.

You can give:

✔ through acts of kindness,

✔ to the needy,

✔ by starting your own ministry,

✔ by contributing your special talents,

✔ by volunteering your time and

✔ by donating money.

Surprise Receiving

A few years ago, our friend Julie and her husband took a group of American high school students on an outreach trip to Haiti. While staying in a small village, the students held Bible clubs for the young children and helped with the construction of much-needed housing for the local residents. Near the end of the trip, a student named Amy received a telephone call from her parents: a fire had destroyed their home. The family was safe and unharmed, but the fire had destroyed all of their possessions.

Even by American standards, Amy's family was considered very wealthy. She was not used to the extreme poverty she witnessed that summer in Haiti. Receiving the disturbing telephone call from home made an already trying situation even more difficult. She had lost everything.

Amy was visibly distraught over her situation. The Haitian girls from her kids' club wondered why she was so sad. When they found out what she had lost, they formed a plan. The girls got together all of the money that they had in the world and gave it to Amy as a farewell gift.

Amy was both grateful and humbled. She could not believe that these young girls, who had so little, cared enough to give her their money so that she could replace some of the things she had lost. She was even more amazed when she saw the size of the contribution. All the money they gave totalled less than she would pay for a nice outfit.

Amy went to Haiti intending to help people who lived in houses made of cardboard and wood scraps. She had come from a mansion, yet in the end, Amy experienced firsthand the amazing true riches of a generous spirit. These young girls had little to give, but they gave it all to help someone they cared about. Who received the greater blessing?

"It is better to give an inexpensive gift with a smile than an expensive one with a frown."

—*Anonymous*

Give from Abundance

Because we live in a society of such abundance, it is so easy to be overwhelmed by all of our stuff. One idea we mentioned in Chapter 3 is the "Two for One" concept. When you (or one of your kids) get something new, give away two things you already have. Just because you don't want something doesn't mean someone else won't be blessed by it.

One author's family recently completed a small remodeling project and got new front doors. The old door was beautiful, but because of the new design, they couldn't use it anymore. They gave their old door to a dear friend who had been recently widowed, and she was thrilled.

Everyday items that many households find unnecessary can be a blessing to others.

- ✔ When you get a new shirt, give away two shirts you never wear. Clothing is appreciated by many charitable organizations.

- ✔ Give unused toys (in good condition) to a local shelter, a children's hospital, or to the struggling family down the street.

- ✔ Children's books, music and videos are great to share with other families after your kids have outgrown them.

- ✔ Coats are always appreciated during the winter months to warm up someone in need.

- ✔ Furniture can be a blessing to that newly married couple just starting out.

- ✔ Yard furniture is always appreciated during the fair weather seasons.

- ✔ Garden tools are a necessity for every home with a yard.

- ✔ Stereo/electronic/video equipment can be a huge perk to a family that has never had this luxury.

✔ **Computers are common in households these days. If you know a home that isn't hooked up to the Internet, perhaps that second computer you have would be a blessing to them.**

Involve your kids in this process as much as possible. Let them see the need others have and develop their own sense of generosity. This may require a little prodding from you. But ultimately your kids will see your example of generosity and follow in your footsteps.

Giving Flows From a Generous Spirit

When David Adamiec was eleven years old, he embarked upon a church project that would impact both his life and the lives of countless children touched by his generosity. His goal was to fill backpacks with personal supplies like clothing and toothbrushes and give them to kids in foster care and protective custody.

David's initial efforts to obtain donated items from a local store did not succeed. Not one to give up, he asked his mother to take him from one store to another. By the end of that year David obtained enough donations to fill fifty backpacks. He then delivered them to a local social services agency, where they were eagerly received.

With the help of his church and community, David has continued his initial effort. His idea has grown into a successful nonprofit with branches in thirteen states. Kidpacks of America has not only distributed thousands of packs nationwide, its reach has also extended as far as Venezuela, Bosnia and Haiti.

Kidpacks has expanded its operation beyond helping kids in foster care. David now reaches out to any kids in need, such as those in shelters. The variety of packs available has also increased. Originally, the three basic backpacks included The Kid Pack, The Activity Pack and The School Pack. The selection has now increased to include Back-to-School and Holiday Toy Packs, which come in a stocking.

Although his original dream has grown, David tries to remain behind the scenes. He says that just imagining the reaction when kids open the backpacks is enough. Yet, in recognition for his work, David has received the Youth of the Year Award from Rotary International and the Hitachi Foundationís Yoshiyama Award. David has also been chosen as an ambassador by the Heart of American Foundation. If your kids are ready to start packing up their own Kidpacks, more information on David's organization is available at **www.kidpacksusa.org**

Time

Time is an incredible gift, and we are all given the same amount. No matter how much money you have, you can't buy more time. Everyone chooses to do different things with their time. It seems that the young never have enough time in their life and as people get older, they have too much time on their hands.

Take time out of your busy life to share with others:

✔ Reconnect with elderly relatives/friends by helping with projects they are unable to do. This is especially great when working alongside others (siblings, cousins, parents, friends).

✔ Visit with a person you know is lonely and needs someone to talk to.

✔ Consider mentoring someone who is going through a difficult time that you yourself once faced. Sharing your learning experiences can be a valuable time for both of you.

✔ Show support for new parents by helping out with some small tasks like folding laundry, taking the baby for a walk or just letting them have a few minutes by themselves.

"In truth, people can generally make time for what they choose to do; it is not really the time but the will that is lacking."
—*Anonymous*

A Lifetime of Giving

A great example of life-long giving is our family friend Lois, who is currently in her nineties. She was widowed well over thirty years ago and now lives in a retirement home. She and her husband never had children of their own, yet Lois has helped raise many mentally challenged kids through her life's work: teaching. Her entire life she has given to others.

Although she no longer drives, she manages to have someone take her to the neighborhood elementary school so she can help teach children to read. As we have watched her over the years, we have always been amazed by what an inspiration she is. She even surfs the Web.

No matter what life deals her she remains positive, always smiling and saying something refreshing. She is always doing something for someone else and always learning. We think that is why she has lived such a long and fruitful life. Lois is a living example of how rewarding life-long generosity can be. Whether young, or just young at heart, all ages can participate and benefit from giving.

> "People who are now old may once have made big contributions to us, earlier in our lives, and have asked nothing in return; you can do something for them now."
> —*Alexandra Stoddard*

Simple Pleasures

Sometimes the simplest things of life bring the most joy to a person. Think of the little things you and your kids can do for others.

Here are just a few ideas:

- ✔ Bake cookies and take them to a friend or neighbor.
- ✔ Give away vegetables from your garden.
- ✔ Send a "Thinking of You" card or handwritten note to someone you haven't talked to in a while.
- ✔ Get your kids to send handwritten notes to someone special (e-mails don't count).

- ✔ Visit an elderly relative or friend. Prepare kids ahead of time with what the environment will be like and what they can say or do.

- ✔ Encourage your kids to write letters and make telephone calls to friends or relatives, sharing the latest family adventures with them.

- ✔ When preparing a meal, get the kids to help. Make a double batch of lasagna and together take the second meal to another family.

- ✔ Have younger kids prepare special artwork for a relative that lives far away.

- ✔ Invite a grandparent to "share" a special event with your family. Examples: school plays, musicals, concerts, fourth of July parades, holiday activities.

- ✔ Bake together at the holidays and give the baked goodies to friends and family.

- ✔ Have children make gifts for grandparents for birthday and holidays (it will be extra work for the kids, but recipients will appreciate them greatly).

Every day we can all find little bits of kindness to brighten someone else's day. Inspire your kids to think of ways they can give encouragement to others and put a smile on their faces. Teach by example. Make it a point to do something nice for someone each day. Remind your kids and yourself: something that seems small and insignificant to you can be big to someone else.

Over and Above the Call

In overwhelmingly difficult circumstances, one family found a way to make a big difference that had farther-reaching effects than they could have ever dreamed. When Kyle Amber was five, his older brother Ian was diagnosed with leukemia. Kyle's parents spent a large amount of time with Ian in the hospital, and Kyle wanted to help, too. Kyle, only in kindergarten at the time, developed a plan. His grandfather was in the printing business and brought home decorative stickers for Kyle, who decided to try and sell the stickers at school as a fundraiser for the hospital. It was a success.

Field Trip Idea:

Senior Home

A senior citizens' home, community or village can be a great place to visit. It is good for your kids as well as the residents who live there. Here are several ideas of good times to visit and some activities you can do while there.

- *Halloween.* Trick-or-treat from door to door. The residents will probably love the entertainment, and it is a safe environment for your kids.

- *Christmas.* Sing carols to the residents. You can even get a group of friends together to join your family. Inquire at the home. They may even have their own choir and you can join them for a sing-a-long.

- *Valentine's Day.* Make special cards for the residents in the home. You can even make decorations for their doors, which have a pleasant impact on everyone's mood.

- *Memorial Day.* Take flags and place them on the doors of the residents. You can even have a fun sing-a-long and sing patriotic songs together.

- *Adopt a Pet.* Go to your local SPCA and adopt a cat or dog to go and live at the home with the seniors. Of course, you need to check with the administrator of the senior home first. Adopting an animal for the home gives the pet a loving environment with lots of people to give love in return. It also serves as great therapy for older people.

Not one to give up, Kyle started a bake sale at his school, which has since turned into an annual event. After the bake sale, his efforts really gained momentum. People in his hometown started to read about his project and began to volunteer more money and toys. Within a year Kyle's idea turned into one of the few volunteer organizations in the country run by kids, for kids, called Kids That Care Pediatric & Cancer Fund.

The entire Amber family is now involved in this fundraising opportunity. Kyle's mom handles the legal and accounting issues. His dad helps by talking with other parents in similar circumstances. Kyle's family considers him the creative one. His dedication increased when his brother's leukemia returned. Ian is currently undergoing intensive chemotherapy, yet when he's feeling well, he plays still plays a major role in Kids That Care. Both Kyle and Ian actively participate in the organization.

Kids That Care has stocked waiting rooms with toys, helped arrange trips for sick children, and given counseling support to kids and parents facing life-threatening illnesses. They even still sell stickers. Who could have known that a boy in kindergarten would develop an idea with such a far-reaching effect? To learn more about Kids That Care email Kyle at **ktckidsthatcare@aol.com.**

"You can give without loving, but you cannot love without giving."
—Amy Carmichael

Needy

There are many groups of people in this world with special needs. If you have a desire to give to others less fortunate than you, there are many organizations that exist. You just need to research a bit to find them.

✔ **Support a child from another country. Allow your kids to help choose who you will support and if possible, request a picture of the child to make it more real for your kids.**

✔ **Save money in a special bank to give for a local fundraiser.**

✔ **Volunteer (with older kids) at a local Habitat for Humanity project.**

✔ **Give regularly to a local cause (shelters, churches, a family in need, etc.).**

✔ **Instead of holding a garage sale, consider giving away many of the items you would normally sell. Consider donating these items to a charity or to friends in need (have the kids help decide what to give).**

✔ **Volunteer to help another family with yard work. (People who are seriously ill, bedridden or disabled especially appreciate this.)**

✔ **Offer to help with housework for a senior citizen confined to his or her home.**

✔ Give new or gently used toys to the children's wing at your local hospital.

✔ Volunteer as a family to help serve/prepare a Christmas or Thanksgiving meal at a local rescue mission.

A Shoe Box Gift

A great example of giving to the needy is sixteen-year-old Kristina, who started a "Shoe Box Ministry." Kristina assembled more than seven hundred packets filled with toiletries and toys for orphans in Armenia. She got the idea from a book she read about a pastor who filled shoe boxes with items for needy children. Kristina gathered donations from churches, community service groups and individuals to create packets for the Armenian children. Even the shipping to Armenia was covered by a corporate donation. The packages were given to each child attending an orphan camp. There were even enough extra packages to donate to two other orphanages.

In Armenia, children are considered orphans if they have one parent or no parents. Because of the country's poor economy, single parents (usually mothers) cannot support their children: many fathers have been killed in the recent armed conflicts.

Kristina learned about the orphan camps in Armenia through her father, a dentist, who volunteers his services every year to the camp. He began his first trip there in 1999. Kristina began going to the camp with her father in 2000, spending four weeks at the camp during the summer of 2002. She plans to extend this project into other geographic areas, as well as expanding the packages to include clothing.

When Kristina started this venture her dad told her he wanted her to "do this right" from the beginning. He had her set up a foundation, put together a board of directors, keep accurate accounting records, develop her own letterhead and do all her own marketing and outreach. They both wanted to keep it a grass-roots ministry.

Kristina was able to accomplish so much due to her perseverance and enjoyment of the process. She has met many interesting people who donated money, time or items. In addition, she has learned valuable business and people skills she will carry with her throughout her life. She has expanded her work to include planting a forest in Armenia. She is currently acquiring a CAT scan machine for Southern Armenia. If you want to learn more about Kristina's ministry you can e-mail her at **shoeboxsharing@yahoo.com.**

Volunteer

Organizations are always on the lookout for committed volunteers. If interested, research local organizations that are looking for people to donate time, talents or specific items to their group. Most are flexible and will welcome any help you can give. Find an organization that provides a service to a needy group you have always wanted to help. Pursue ways you and your family can assist them.

Consider these organizations:

- ✔ **Churches**
- ✔ **Youth Centers**
- ✔ **Retirement Homes**
- ✔ **YMCA/YWCA**
- ✔ **Hospitals**
- ✔ **Hospice**
- ✔ **Schools**
- ✔ **Libraries**
- ✔ **Museums**
- ✔ **Zoos**

If you don't know of resources in your area that welcome volunteers, check out these websites for more information. Some of these sites can link you to their local organizations by your ZIP code.

- ✔ **www.give.org**
- ✔ **www.helping.org**
- ✔ **www.idealist.org**
- ✔ **www.independentsector.org**

✔ www.nvoad.org

✔ www.volunteermatch.org

✔ www.charities.org

✔ www.charityamerica.com

"Philanthropy, like charity, must begin at home."
—*Charles Lamb*

Out of the Shadows

When he was just twelve years old, NFL quarterback Brian Griese lost his mother to breast cancer. At that time, he felt very alone, as if he was the only twelve-year-old boy in the world whose mother had died. He didn't feel like he could talk with anybody about his feelings.

When he was a Denver Bronco, Brian started a foundation for grieving children and families in honor and in memory of his mother, Judith Ann Griese. The sponsorship money he was to receive never touched his hands. It went directly to the Judith Ann Griese Foundation.

Brian spent his off days and off seasons huddled with Denver's social and civic leaders. He asked for their money, their time and their energy. He enlisted their support to serve on his foundation's board of directors. When not working in Denver, he was often in some other city working to create a national organization around the issue of grief and loss.

Brian is as concerned about helping children and families who have lost a loved one as he is with playing in another Super Bowl. Many athletes and celebrities form foundations for show, for image, for tax shelters, for all the wrong reasons. Brian's interest is as real as his scars, yet he doesn't broadcast this to those around him. Without anyone in the Broncos' organization knowing, he wrote the foundation's mission statement in April 2001. Since then, he has immersed himself in bringing it to life.

Brian feels that kids can help kids, since they speak the same language. The cornerstone of the foundation is Judi's House which provides a safe and comfortable atmosphere where grieving children and their families can express the thoughts and feelings associated with the loss of a loved one. Judi's House gives kids a place to go to where they are not alone with their grief.

115

If you want further information about the Judith Ann Griese Foundation for Grieving Children and Families, go to **www.judithanngriesefoundation.org** or **www.judishouse.org.**

Brian Griese's desire to help others is admirable, yet he is not driven by public perception. He did not begin the foundation to create a better public persona for himself. His motivation comes from a genuine and personal desire to help kids as they face a tragedy that he too experienced.

Giving Plan

Giving is a personal thing: something that, unless such publicity benefits the particular cause, should not be broadcast to the world. If you give for the purpose of getting accolades from others, you're probably giving for the wrong reasons. Evaluate why it is important for your family to give. Be sure to get input from your kids so they understand the importance of their involvement in both family and individual giving.

- ✔ **Does your family have long-term and short-term giving goals?**

- ✔ **Who are you currently giving to?**

- ✔ **Who do your kids want to give to in the future?**

- ✔ **What is your criteria for identifying a need?**

- ✔ **Do you have flexibility in your plan to help out with emergency needs to others? (It is a good idea to set aside a small amount of money for the flexibility category.)**

A great way to prioritize your giving is to write each group, individual or cause on an index card along with how much you give. Spread the cards out on a table. Discuss, as a family, who is getting what type of help and why. After talking with all family members, you may find the approach to your giving plan is clear. However, you may need to add some new categories or make a few adjustments.

What Do You Value?

While preparing your family Giving Plan, take the time to evaluate your wealth. What is true wealth and what really is financial freedom?

Remember, how many things you have, how much you save, or how you spend your money does not define your meaning in life. Your real treasures are those around you: your family, friends and especially your children.

"Never lose a chance of saying a kind word."

—*William Makepeace Thackeray*

1. Teach your kids about what life is like for children in other countries. Without becoming too preachy, remind them how fortunate we are to live in a country where we enjoy so much freedom and abundance.

2. Involve your kids in family giving. Allow them to help pick out some of the "gently used" items (toys, clothes, etc.) that your family will donate.

3. Contribute monetarily to local and national charities and fundraisers. Encourage your kids to learn about these organizations. Find out who founded them, what their purpose is, and who the money will be distributed to.

4. Encourage your kids to come up with their own ideas about giving. As this chapter has shown, kids can come up with some pretty inspirational ways to give both their time and money to help others.

5. Do you remember when thirty seemed old? Teach your kids to respect those who are older than they are, whether they are thirty or ninety. Plan an occasional family event to visit an elderly relative or family friend. Just hearing stories of your day-to-day life will be a treasured gift.

6. Teach your kids to give both spontaneously and within the limits of a plan. Allow them to be part of an overall family plan for giving.

7. Create a blessings chart/poster or bulletin board to remind your family daily of all you are sharing with others. Let each family member participate in creating this masterpiece. It can include items such as pictures, articles, artwork or mementos.

8. Make a day of it and volunteer at a Habitat for Humanity building project in your community.

9. Mow an elderly neighbor's lawn.

10. Have your kids help prepare and deliver a meal to a family with a new baby.

11. Set up giving traditions. This is especially fun around the holidays. Ideas:

    ✔ Donate a turkey to your local rescue mission at Thanksgiving.

    ✔ Have your older kids help serve a holiday dinner at a soup kitchen.

    ✔ Find a local church with a shoe box ministry and pick a child to buy for each year.

    ✔ Contribute coats to a local school or charity that distributes them to children in need.

    ✔ Find a new family in need to help every year.

Conclusion

"Mooo...tivation"

● ●

Congratulations! By finishing this book you have joined the ranks of those who want to create a better financial future for their kids. While this is the final chapter, it is not the end. In fact, just the opposite is true. This is only the beginning. You are now at the starting point as you empower your family with all of the resources available to you.

The subtitle of this book is *The Guide to Financial Freedom at Any Age!* What is financial freedom? Is it just about money? Financial freedom is wealth: wealth in practical knowledge, experience and wisdom. As you exercise your financial freedom, you will use that knowledge and experience to develop control over money and not allow money to control you. This is financial freedom!

This wealth will not occur overnight. Yet by integrating the examples and incorporating the ideas in this book you can develop a new mindset that will allow you to see beyond the traditional constraints of saving and investing. In doing so, you will find ways to more effectively communicate with your kids about financial matters and together explore the field of financial freedom.

By empowering your kids with a sound financial foundation, you will help them make good financial choices and keep them from becoming ensnared by their need to make money. Instead, this foundation will enable them to develop the skills necessary to have their money work for them.

As the many creative people we described throughout this book illustrate, there are myriad paths to financial freedom. We are confident that as you apply the principles discussed throughout *CashCow Kids™*, you will be empowered to help your children transform their dreams into real-life business opportunities as you shape your family's future financial success.

The Path Less Traveled

You are now at a fork in the road.

One path will take you back to the old way of thinking. Initially, you may find comfort in the familiar surroundings. However, your feelings of comfort will fade as you begin to realize that financial constraints are once again limiting your choices. As you lead your family down this path, you will perpetuate the cycle of financial bondage.

*"The last of the human freedoms:
to choose one's attitude in any given set of circumstances,
to choose one's own way."*
—*Viktor Frankl*

The other path will take you forward to a whole new perspective on money and financial matters. You will soon discover that money is not a limitation, but a tool your entire family can use to find the greener pastures. You will find an unlimited number of ways to guide your kids on their paths to freedom by helping them pursue their own dreams, create their own opportunities and develop their own cash cows.

Regardless of your background or age, this is a choice only you can make. We are confident you will choose wisely as you and your kids move forward to an entirely new outlook on your financial future. We wish you all the best as you venture out and stake your claim in your new financial frontier!

See ya outside the pasture!

Money Making Ideas

Traditional money makers, like babysitting and yard services, are great. However, don't forget to consider other options available to your kids, which can be more creative or innovative. Their imaginations can often take them places you would never consider. Consider some of the many options:

Author

Write a book. The market for young authors is hot right now. Publishers are always looking for up-and-coming writing talent. Help them get their feet in the door by joining writing associations or attending local and regional seminars and conferences. Seminars are a great setting to network with other authors, agents and publishers. The exposure can be invaluable.

Babysitter With a Twist

There are many variations of babysitting services your kids can offer. Below are just a few creative ideas to help your kids provide unique services. A few suggestions to help make their services more valuable and appear more responsible would be to have business cards made. These can be very creative and cute. In addition, research infant and child CPR certification and babysitting courses offered through local agencies or hospitals. It will definitely give them credibility if they can participate in these courses.

Babysitting drop-off: Help your kids start their new venture by opening your home to young children three days a week from three to five. Moms can go run a couple of errands and the kids get to play! Your kids can take sign-ups and have a limit. To get the word out, encourage them to distribute fliers in your neighborhood or to friends with young children. Charge a flat hourly rate per child.

Babysitting for the weekend: Parents of young children often find it difficult to find time away together, even if it is for one night. Providing a service so the parents feel comfortable leaving for the weekend or overnight can be a big bonus. Of course, this job would include feeding, bathing and maybe even driving the kids to activities. Part of the job description could include losing sleep if those little tikes don't sleep through the night or are very early risers. A good way to find families that would need this service is from current babysitting clients, word of mouth, friends and family. A bonus for this service would be to charge a flat weekend rate, not hourly. Discuss the specifics with each family regarding food, expenses, etc.

This idea also works well for families with children who are old enough to stay by themselves for a few hours but not overnight. Your older teenager can then act as a weekend companion to supervise activities, meals and such.

Babysitting companion: When new parents have several little ones, a companion for the older kids is sometimes helpful. Offer your services to parents who will be home but need to complete several tasks they just can't seem to finish with the kids around.

Bike Mechanic

Are your kids experts when it comes to fixing their own bikes? Why not encourage them to help others out and make money at the same time? They could have a traveling tool kit and make house calls to fix those flat tires, brakes, etc. Or they could have standing hours of operation and work out of the family garage.

Chores for Elderly

If your kids are willing to do some of the tasks we take for granted, many older people have a need for their services. A good place to start is at a senior residential village or complex. Help them advertise their services or spread the word by customer recommendations.

We have a friend whose eighty-five-year-old grandma has problems with her sciatica and can't do the simple task of vacuuming her carpet. So, once a week she pays someone ten dollars a visit to vacuum her apartment, which is about eight hundred square feet: a simple fifteen- to twenty-minute job once a week.

This type of service has a lot of potential if your kids can find the right clients. Ideally, they will find clients who live in close proximity to make it more time-efficient and cost-effective. This could be the perfect after-school business.

Cleaning Services

Your kids can offer cleaning services for businesses, homes, after party clean-up or any type of special circumstance in which they see an opportunity. One teen saw the opportunity with the new subdivision of homes being built across the street from her. She approached the developer to do a deep cleaning of the new house to remove the construction dirt and scraps before the new owners moved in.

Maybe your kids hate doing their chores at home, but getting paid for doing them is completely different! They could offer complete house-cleaning services, or specialize in one or more areas, such as attic/basement/garage clean-ups. Their services could be utilized weekly, monthly or as needed. Your kids could then charge clients a flat rate for each visit.

Clown for Hire (Kids' Parties)

Do your kids like to make other kids laugh? Help them become clowns for younger kids' parties. They will need to have a good routine with a few fun tricks. It will improve their business if they can learn to make balloon animals or something cute the kids can take home with them. (Customers will think they got their money's worth if the clown leaves something with the kids.) Your kids can charge a flat rate per party. Remind them to find out ahead of time the number of kids who will attend and also to talk to the parents in charge about their expectations.

Computer/Office Tasks

Many businesses need assistance completing the mundane tasks of applying labels, stuffing envelopes, collating, etc. This is a great after-school and evening type of project. Most copy shops charge per hour for the labor to complete such tasks. Your kids can bid jobs by the hour or charge the customer a flat rate.

Computer Tutor/Web Site Development Service

Are your kids whizes with computers and the Web? Many adults are not, and they make good customers for a business helping people learn to use PCs and develop Web sites for their families or businesses.

Contestant in Story, Poem, Art Contests

Do your kids love to write or draw? A whole world awaits their talents. Local, state and national contests of all sorts are always popping up. Keep your feelers out for these opportunities, which could open doors to the writing and art world for your young authors and artists.

Cook for Hire

If you can't keep your kids out of the kitchen, they could start a catering business. Let them cook meals for the elderly and busy parents, or offer cooking lessons to all ages. If they already have a collection of fabulous recipes, why not have them write a cookbook?

Craft Show Exhibitor

Do your kids have a special type of craft they like to make? It could be woodworking, wreaths, needle craft, candles or really anything they love to make that people would want to buy. Research local craft fairs in your area. If your kids make the rounds on selling at fairs throughout the year, they may be able to make money during the craft fair season. Be sure they get information on all fees, set-up costs and include all their material costs when they establish a sales price on their products. If a booth rental is cost-prohibitive, they could team up with some other crafters and split the costs. If you are creative in your research, you may be able to find fairs that don't charge participants.

Create Fliers, Invitations, Announcements

Many adults do not have computer abilities to create even the simplest type of document. If your kids are computer experts and like doing this type of work, they could offer this service to the computer illiterate.

Dance Instructor

If your kids have years of dancing or gymnastics under their belts, giving lessons could be the perfect business for them. If they have a place to hold the classes (such as a garage, church facility, etc.) and the equipment for music, other expenses should be minimal. Dance away!

Errand or Messenger Service

This idea works well in larger cities where there are more people and public transportation. Many people need help with all sorts of errands in these busy times.

A friend of ours had a great side business working as a personal assistant, helping busy executives and parents with their personal errands.

Food Delivery

Many offices are so busy that it's difficult for employees to get out for lunch. Your kids could start a delivery service for busy people. They can start taking orders mid-morning and deliver meals by lunch time. Charge for the food plus a delivery charge per person. They might also offer a break service where they bring in pastries and drinks in the morning and afternoon. If they do business with a few select restaurants, they might be able to negotiate a cheaper rate or at least get orders processed more quickly. This would be a great summer job or business for college-age kids where their school schedules are more flexible.

Gift Wrapping Service

This can be a service year round, but could explode during the holidays. Your kids provide all the materials such as boxes, wrapping, bows, ribbon, etc. Charge customers a flat fee per package. Be sure to include all the material costs plus labor in the final price. They can pick up and deliver the packages as an added perk to their customers.

Kids' Book Club

This is a great idea for the summer. Have a Summer Reading Club for whatever age group your kids are comfortable. Pick age-appropriate books and activities. Have the kids meet at your house once a week to discuss the books and do the activities or crafts that coordinate with their reading. Your kids can charge parents a flat fee for participating in the club or a weekly rate as they attend each meeting. This can be a lot of fun for all involved.

Holiday Helper

There are so many ways to make money during the different holidays throughout the year:

Christmas: Provide a decorating service to put up and take down Christmas trees, household decorations, outside lights . . . you get the idea. Providing a time-saving service during a busy season can be a huge help to families as well as businesses. Advertise through fliers, friends, family and word of mouth. Your kids need to be organized to pull this off, because they'll have many of their own deadlines around the same time. Time management and delegation is the key to making a business like this work.

Annual holidays: Think about all the holidays throughout the year besides Christmas that require a little extra thought. Perhaps your kids' service could be providing decorations, baking cookies for the holiday, making special cards, gift baskets or such.

- ✔ Presidents Day
- ✔ Valentines Day
- ✔ Easter
- ✔ May Day
- ✔ Mother's Day
- ✔ Memorial Day
- ✔ Father's Day
- ✔ Fourth of July
- ✔ Labor Day
- ✔ Halloween
- ✔ Thanksgiving

House Sitter

This can involve many different things and can vary in length. The key is to be flexible for clients and really serve their needs. Clients with pets might require more time than those who just needd the mail and paper brought into the house. Finding a reliable person who can handle this type of responsibility is great, and as friends and neighbors like your kids' service, they can ask them to spread the word.

For college students, especially, long-term house sitting can be great for a family leaving for the summer, a long vacation or special circumstances such as a sabbatical. Not only might they be paid for their time, but they can also live rent-free!

Internet Research

Provide the service of finding information for businesses or individuals on the Web. Researching a specific topic can be very time consuming. If your kids are a whiz at finding information on the Web, this is up their alley. Be sure they have specific information from the client on the exact information they need. They could charge clients hourly or a flat rate. They should have a good idea before they start a project of how much time it will take them to research.

Magician for Hire (Kids' Parties)

Do your kids have magical talents? Being a birthday party magician for parties could be the right business for them. They need to have a good show with some pizzazz, perhaps live bunnies or something fun for the kids. Once they've done a few parties, their bookings should grow. Be sure to take their business cards to each party and spread them around.

Note: Be careful about the live rabbits; they tend to grow and multiply quickly. A friend once had a magic act, and his bunnies kept outgrowing the magical box into which they were suppose to disappear!

Music Instructor

Are your kids good music students? They could give lessons to others and provide the added service of going to clients' homes, which could help a lot of parents' busy schedules.

Newsletter Service

Many companies or organizations send monthly newsletters. Providing a layout, copy, graphics, collating, mailing labels and distribution service could grow into a great business. This is a great business for journalism students. Their journalism friends may also want to help as the business expands.

Painting Service

If your kids have some experience with painting they might consider this type of business. People are always renovating and need a good, reasonably priced painter. They could paint exteriors in the nicer months and interiors during the colder months.

Party Planner

Do your kids love parties? They could be a party planner for any type of party. They would take care of everything from invitations, organizing games, food, decorations, prizes and entertainment. They could charge clients either hourly or a flat rate per event.

Party Server

Maybe your kids don't like planning a party but like to help out more behind the scenes. They can offer to be a server. Their duties would be to arrive at the party early to help set up or prepare food, serve food as guests arrive and host them throughout the party. Afterward, they assist in the clean-up. Clients could be charged per event or by the hour.

Pet Sitting

Pet sitting for vacationers can cross over into the house-sitting area also. When someone is gone overnight, Fido needs to be fed, walked, bathed and loved. This can be a great money making venture on an as-needed basis. Once your kids get the word out to neighbors and friends, they should have a steady clientele.

Pet Walking

Perhaps the little old lady down the street can't get out to walk her dog regularly, or the family next door doesn't have time to fit a dog walk into their busy schedules. Clients can be charged an hourly rate for this service.

Puppeteer

Have a traveling puppet show for entertaining kids. Your kids can travel to birthday parties, school carnivals, church events or special parties. Have a strong show with some fun puppets kids universally like.

Rummage Sales

Garage sales of old toys, clothes, videos and books are always popular. Your kids could hold a standing sale the first Saturday of every month. They could spend time between sales collecting merchandise from friends and family or just doing cleaning around your house. They also can provide a service to families having their own sales by selling kits to get their event organized and underway. It can be overwhelming to take on the task of putting together a garage sale, especially if the family is moving or selling a sizable amount of merchandise. Providing the service of helping them organize, set–up and price and organize the merchandise can be a big help.

Sales

Your kids could sell refreshments at their siblings' soccer games, baseball games, etc. If they like to sell, help them look for opportunities to sell a product. Sales opportunities are all around us.

Scrapbook Creator

If your kids have creative talents, providing a scrapbook service to busy parents could be just the answer. Parents give your kids the pictures they want in the scrap book, and your kids go for it. The benefit of this business is that they can work on the projects on their own time. They can either charge a flat rate or price per page. Be sure they figure in the cost of all their materials.

A friend had a part-time, fourteen-year-old babysitter who was in the middle of her summer break. Our friend had given her about all the babysitting hours she could stand, but she was still bored. She is a very creative person and when asked if she wanted to create a baby book, she jumped at the opportunity. The mom bought all the materials and paid her a flat fee for doing the book. She had a blast doing the scrapbook and created quite a memento. This busy mom felt like a bad mom for not having the time to do her first son's baby book, but the problem was solved! How many other moms haven't had the time to make their kids' scrapbooks?

Shopping Service

Do your kids love to shop and spend someone else's money? A shopping service could be the perfect business for them. Many busy families do not have time to even go to the grocery store. Their service could include shopping for everyday items as well as birthday gifts, special holidays or occasions.

Sign Service

Look around the community and see all the signs that exist. They are everywhere from the local shopping center to the large super stores, businesses, small and large need signs. In addition many organizations at school, church, etc. need signs. The advanced technology of computers these days makes generating signs easy. If your kids have access to the proper equipment and have skills in graphic design, a sign business could be perfect for them. They could charge customers a flat rate per job, depending on the size of the sign.

Story Teller

If your kids love to read and tell stories to little kids, have a standing time each week for story hour. Parents can bring their kids, for a small fee, to hear their stories, sing a few songs, maybe color and eat a snack. This is a great idea as a neighborhood project.

Swim Instructor

If your kids are strong swimmers, encourage them to get the proper certifications to teach private or group swim lessons. It is a great summer business. They could offer the benefit of going to the client's homes to give the lessons. They need to decide age groups and the type of lessons they want to offer. If they're good with time management, they could schedule lessons so they work only part of the summer or half-days.

Travel Kit Creator

Make travel kits for families going on vacation with kids. Any amount of time riding in a car can be too long for little children. A good way to pass the time is to keep them busy doing something. Make bags full of fun stuff. For example, our friends' kids will play with pipe cleaners for hours. They have contests who can make the funniest animal. Paperclip chains are always fun, too. Make a game they can play in the car: auto BINGO or the Alphabet License Plate game. Your kids can fill the bags with all kinds of imagination-sparking stuff. They can charge a flat rate per bag and get the word out to potential clients before the vacation season.

Typing Service

Believe it or not, many people young and old cannot type. If your kids are expert typists they can offer a typing service. This service can include preparation of term papers, newsletters, business letters, personal letters, resumes, just about anything your client could need typed. Charge by the hour or the page.

Technology Expert

If you're kids are a whiz on the computer or with some type of technical equipment, encourage them to sell their services to other people who are not so technically inclined. For example, they can create homemade movies using a digital camera, record television programming using a VCR, or load photographs onto CDs.

Tutor

Do your kids love a particular subject in school? Maybe they can share their expertise with others by tutoring them in that subject. You could have the students come to them or provide the added service of going to their house. Tutors can make great money, while at the same time really help someone in need of the knowledge.

Web Shepherd

Have you visited a website you swear hasn't been updated since 1998? Well, there could be some great opportunities in this market. If your kids are Web savvy, they can offer their services to local businesses that never quite understood that a successful website needs to change. Have your kids be on the look-out for businesses in the area and pitch their services to them.

Summertime Fun Expert

Parents and kids have more free time on their hands during summer vacation. They are always looking for fun things to do. Why not have your kids create a list of resources of activities and events in your area they can do. List as much free stuff as you can find; everyone likes to save money. Kids can do their research during the spring and have your pamphlet printed right before school is out of session. They can market the brochure at schools, churches and social organizations. This concept would also work well for other times of the year, such as the winter holidays, fall activities or spring events. Once they get their information sources established, then they can make contact four times a year, update the information, and go to print. They can keep the publication simple and at a reasonable price. If they sell volume, the cost of printing will be drastically reduced.

Yard Worker

If your kids like to mow lawns, trim hedges and rake leaves they are in business. So many people have little free time, and this is a great kid business constantly in demand. They can start by asking around to get an idea of current rates then work with friends, family and neighbors as their first clients. They can eventually network to get more business. They'll need a lawn mower and some yard tools. If you live in a house, you probably already have these items they could use. If they don't have access to equipment, they can offer to do people's yard with the client's equipment at a discount. Then they can save up to buy their own equipment. Remember services can include weekly maintenance, quarterly clean-up, weeding, special projects, raking leaves, watering. In the winter they could shovel snow, if you live in that type of climate.

appendix B

Talking Points

Many aspects of life involve money in some way or another, providing lots of opportunities throughout the day to talk to your kids about money. We have put together a list of situations where good discussion about money could occur.

Acquaintances

Whenever you run into a friend or an acquaintance who has been able to succeed in a given profession, talk to your kids about what that person does to earn a living. Discuss the pros and cons of that type of business, what type of education it requires, why the friend has succeeded, and how he or she got there. Talking about someone's attributes/strengths will give your kids a good standard for analyzing interests and professions they might like to pursue. As you respectfully describe others and their successes, you will be conveying a standard of conduct to your kids while you help expose them to a creative business idea.

Bill Paying Party

Paying the bills is not a fun task. However, it is a monthly/weekly ritual that must be done. So why not make the best of it and have some fun? It seems that whenever parents sit down to pay the bills, the kids gravitate to the dining room table and want to help. Let the kids join the party, get out their calculators and write those checks. If you have young children, let them write pretend checks and play with the calculators. If your kids are older, let them write a couple of checks and do some calculations for you.

Just don't forget to sign the checks yourself!

Church

Most churches are completely dependent on giving. If you attend church or some type of worship facility, talk to your kids about how some of the aspects of the church are similar to a business. Explain how they have bills, expenses such as utilities, employees, etc. Also discuss the differences between a church and a business.

Daycare/Babysitter

If your kids have a regular nanny, babysitter or even an occasional babysitter, talk to them about it. Let them understand the costs involved with these types of services, the kinds of skills the provider needs and the general reason your family chooses to use each specific person.

Driving

Talk about why you drive a certain type of vehicle. Discuss how you purchased it. Why do you buy used cars? Or why do you buy brand new cars?

Entertainment

The entertainment field is so broad you could talk about it for days. When you go to the movies, talk to your kids not only about the stars in the film but about all the behind-the-scenes people involved in making a movie: the set designers, the costume designers, make-up artists, producers, casting people, directors, to name a few. Talk about how these people make their money and how they probably got into the business. Of course, there are other types of entertainment activities besides the movies. Identify them and discuss all their money-related aspects.

Errands

While out and about on errands, discuss all the different services your family relies on for everyday life. How do those businesses rely on your family to support them so they can support their families? List those businesses you use on a daily, weekly, monthly and semi-annual basis.

Extra-Curricular Activities

Written into the job description of every parent is the responsibility of shuttling kids to and fro, from home to their various activities. Identify the lessons or activities your family participates in such as swimming, tennis golf, music, dance or gymnastics. This list can be endless. Discuss the reason you encourage your kids to pursue these interests. If you choose to talk about how much those lessons, and the extras involved, cost, don't forget to remind them of the benefits of these activities. An enlightening practice is to let them list what they think the benefits are before you suggest ideas of your own.

Family Meetings

Use these gatherings to help create family unity. Hold regular family meetings to discuss important financial business. Identify a standing time for all family members to be present. You can discuss budget issues, clothing funds, allowances if you give them, why the family is cutting back in certain areas, investment opportunities, etc. This is a great time to identify goals and be supportive as team players for the family, as well as to develop support for one another in individual endeavors.

Free Activities

A fun activity is to make a list of all the things your family can do for free. Your kids will have a ball doing the research, and you will be surprised by some of the great ideas your family will have. Look for a local publication that identifies free activities in your community. If one is not available, creating one could be a future business idea for one of your kids.

Grandparents/Elderly

When you leave their grandparents or when visiting an elderly person, talk to your kids about the concept of retirement. Discuss what retirement means, how retired people live if they aren't actively working, what those people did to earn money so they could retire. The whole idea of retirement changes with each generation. Research this concept as a family. You might even ask your grandparents what retirement meant when they were younger.

Also, keep in mind that the word retirement doesn't mean the person has to be elderly. It's not uncommon for people to retire in their early thirties and forties. Talk to kids about the concept of reaching goals early, having plenty of money and retiring at an early age.

Grocery Store

The weekly or sometimes daily trips to the grocery store can be a great learning experience for all family members. Pointing out the costs of the items you purchase can teach kids a lot. Bring along a calculator for each kid. Let them calculate the cost of each item and realize how much it costs to run a household. Yet, with younger kids, don't overwhelm them with the costs. At any age, the point isn't to make them worry about how much you spend, just to help them become more aware of some of the costs involved.

Laundry Time

Let's be honest: This is not a fun topic, but the fact is every household has dirty clothes. Yes, every day we wear garments that need to be cleaned, dried, ironed and put away. Then we start the whole process all over again. Talk to your kids as they help you sort the clothes, wash, dry and fold them. List all of the items necessary to this process, such as electricity, gas, detergents, water and all of the other components that are needed to do the laundry.

Meal Time

Where did the food come from that you are eating? How did you buy it? Who delivered the food to the store? Identify all the different type of businesses it took to get your food on the table. How does your family earn money to support your lifestyle?

Milestones

One of the great joys of life is celebrating the milestones along the way, including birthdays, anniversaries, weddings, baptisms and special parties. Especially when they are older, this is a great opportunity to talk with kids about money.

Weddings are a great example. Generally, events don't get much bigger than a wedding, and some families spare no expense. Any time you are invited to a wedding provides an opportunity to talk about your family's philosophy on big events. Explain why or why not you like to spend lots of money on something like a wedding. Explain how it is a personal decision and differs for each family. Some families save their entire life for such an event, while some seek passive income opportunities to pay for it. Some families keep these important events simple, whether by choice or necessity, yet still manage to celebrate in a big way.

Caution: As in many other areas, do not make money (whether the amount of or the lack of) the focus of any of these events. The last thing you want to do is make your child feel guilty about the cost of his birthday party or gift.

Outside Services

Every family has numerous services they use outside the home, such as hairstylists, cleaners, insurance agents, lawyers, doctors, dentists, pharmacies, gas stations, car washes and so on. Talk to your kids about each of these professions. Discuss their possible educational backgrounds and training. Discuss why the particular service is successful.

Restaurant

Whenever you go out to eat with the family, talk about why you choose a particular restaurant. Have your kids look at the costs of the different meals. Don't forget to point out the different kids' meals available.

Retail Shopping

Shopping for items such as clothes with your kids can be exhilarating or exasperating, depending on how demanding or particular your children are. Talk to your kids about why you shop at certain stores, the types of clothing they carry, the value you get for your clothes.

Services that Come to You

List all the services your household uses, such as a gardener, house cleaning service, plumber, appliance repair, carpet cleaner, window washer, babysitter, newspaper delivery person, or grocery delivery service. Calculate the cost-effectiveness and discuss the convenience of each of these services for your family.

Television Time

Watching commercials gives a perfect opportunity to identify all kinds of topics to talk about related to money. Talk about the product for sale, the marketing of the product, the advertising style, the company, the concept and all of the people and businesses related to that one product.

Warehouse Shopping

Shopping trips at bulk warehouse stores give you a chance to talk about cost savings with your kids. Is it really a savings or do people only think it is because the items are sold in a warehouse? Let them do some calculations and figure it out. Help them consider how much of the stuff you buy at these stores are necessities and how much are just "I wants." There is nothing wrong with items that aren't necessities; it is just important to distinguish between the two.

appendix **C**

Recommended Reading

Defined by Age Category If Appropriate

Kids

101 Marvelous Money Making Ideas for Kids by Heather Wood

American Girl Library Moneymakers by Ingrid Roper

Growing Money: A Complete (And Completely Updated) Investing Guide for Kids by Gail Karlitz, et al.

If You Made a Million by Adriane G. Berg

Kid Cash by Joe Lamancusa

Kids, Parents & Money by Willard Stawski II

Money Sense for Kids! by Hollis Page Harman

Neale S. Godfrey's Ultimate Kids' Money Book by Neale S. Godfrey

Smart Money Moves for Kids by Judith Briles

The Kids' Allowance Book by Am Nathan, Debbie Palen

The Kids' Guide to Money by Steve Otfinoski

The Totally Awesome Business Book for Kids by Adriane G. Berg and Arthur Berg Bochner

Totally Awesome Money/Business Book Pakfor Kids by Arthur Berg Bochner

Teens

Complete Idiot's Guide to Money for Teens by Susan Shelly

How to Go to College Almost for Free by Ben Kaplan

Money Matters for Teens by Larry Burkett, Marnie Wooding (Contributor)

Money Matters for Teens Workbook: Age 15–18 by Larry Burkett, Todd Temple (Contributor)

The 7 Habits of Highly Effective Teens by Sean Covey

The Lazy Youth's Road to Success by A. J. Yager

The Motley Fool Investment Guide for Teens: 8 Steps to Having More Money Than Your Parents Ever Dreamed of by David Gardner ,et al

Whiz Teens in Business by Danielle Vallee

College

How I Retired at 26! A Step-by-Step Guide to Accessing Your Freedom and Wealth at Any Age by Asha Tyson

Please Send Money! by Dara Duguay

The One Minute Millionaire by Mark Victor Hansen and Robert G. Allen

The Young Entrepreneur's Edge by Jennifer Kushell

The Young Entrepreneur's Guide to Starting and Running a Business by Steve Mariotti

Parents/Grandparents

105 Questions Children Ask About Money Matters: With Answers from the Bible for Busy Parents by Larry Burkett, et al.

A Mind at a Time by Mel Levine, M.D.

Finance from Piggy Bank to Prom by Willard Stawski

Kids' Allowances—How Much, How Often & How Come, A Guide for Parents by David McCurrach

Money Doesn't Grow on Trees by Ellie Kay

Money Grows on Trees: How to Make, Manage, and Master Money by Alton H. Howard, Sam Walton

Rich Kid Smart Kid by Robert T. Kiyosaki and Sharon L. Lechter, CPA

The Allowance Workbook for Kids and Their Parents by David McCurrach

The Totally Awesome Money Book for Kids (And Their Parents) by Adriane G. Berg and Arthur Berg, Bochner (Introduction)

General

Achieving Financial Liberty by Robert G. Allen

Building Wealth by Dolf de Roos, Ph.D.

Conversations with Millionaires by Mike Litman, et al.

Creating Wealth by Robert G. Allen

Dolf on Property by Dolf de Roos, Ph.D.

Extraordinary Profits from Ordinary Properties by Dolf de Roos, Ph.D.

God Wants You to Be Rich by Paul Zane Pilzer

How to Win Friends and Influence People by Dale Carnegie

If You Want to Be Rich & Happy, Don't Go to School by Robert T. Kiyosaki

Keys to Success by Napoleon Hill

Mortgage Magic by Dolf de Roos, Ph.D.

Multiple Streams of Income by Robert G. Allen

Rich Dad Poor Dad by Robert T. Kiyosaki

Rich Dad's Cashflow Quadrant by Robert T. Kiyosaki and
     Sharon L. Lechter
Rich Dad's Guide to Investing by Robert T. Kiyosaki and
     Sharon L. Lechter
Rich Dad's Prophecy by Robert T. Kiyosaki and Sharon L. Lechter
Rich Dad's Protecting Your #1 Asset by Michael A. Lechter, Esq.
Rich Dad's Real Estate Riches by Dolf de Roos, Ph.D.
Rich Dad's Retire Young, Retire Rich by Robert T. Kiyosaki and
     Sharon Lechter
Rich Dad's Sales Dogs by Blair Singer
Riches Within Your Reach by Robert Collier
Richest Man in Babylon by George Clason
Success Through a Positive Mental Attitude by Napoleon Hill, and
     W. Clement Stone
The One Minute Millionaire by Mark Victor Hansen and Robert G. Allen
The Power of Focus by Jack Canfield, et al.
Think and Grow Rich by Napoleon Hill
Unlimited Wealth by Paul Zane Pilzer

appendix

D

Websites

Defined by Age If Appropriate

Parents

www.bankrate.com
www.finishrich.com
www.richdad.com
www.smartgrandparenting.com

Kids

www.bigchange.com
www.catalogcity.com
www.coolbank.com
www.deca.org
www.edu4kids.com/money
www.heathereducational.com
www.independentmeans.com
www.kidsbank.com
www.kidshalloffame.com
www.kidsmoney.com
www.kidsmoneycents.com
www.kidssenseonline.com
www.strongkids.com
www.kidsmoney.org
www.kidsbank.com
www.richkidsmartkid.com
www.strongkids.com
www.youngbiz.com
www.youngentrepreneur.com

Teens

www.coolbank.com
www.kolbe.com
www.lifeforce.com
www.nfte.com
www.scholarshipcoach.com
www.yeo.org
www.youngbiz.com

College

www.aba.com
www.cardratings.org
www.consumerjungle.org
www.financial-education-icfe.org
www.frugalliving.com
www.keip.org
www.moneymangement.org

Giving

www.charities.org
www.give.org
www.helping.org
www.idealist.org
www.indepdendentsector.org
www.nvoad.org
www.volunteermatch.org

Acknowledgments

. . . .

Many people deserve our gratitude and appreciation. We gratefully acknowledge all those who have helped us along the way.

First, we thank our husbands. They have been our biggest supporters and their constant encouragement has been priceless. Now it is your turn, guys!

We also thank our very own CashCow Kids for putting up with sleep-deprived and sometimes distracted moms. You have been real troopers! We couldn't have written this book without you. We wouldn't have written this book without you.

Thank you, too, to everyone who helped with the tangible production of this book. Specifically, we thank our book designer, Peri Poloni of Knockout Design. Your help has been invaluable as you have patiently dealt with our many questions and changes. To Karen Risch of Just Write Literary & Editorial Partners: Your assistance in clarifying and rewriting our manuscript has been superb.

To Dan Poynter: Your assistance in helping us bring this book from creative thought to final product and beyond has been invaluable.

We are truly thankful for the many individuals and organizations who contributed to the conceptual development of this book including, but not limited to: David Adameic, Robert G. Allen, Kyle Amber, Richard K. Anderson, Michelle Anton, Jr., Cynthia and John Appleby, John Assaraf, Emily and Hillary Benedict, Vicki Benedict, Olivia Bennett, Larry Burkett, Lore Callahan, Jack Canfield, Janice Cavalla, George Clason, Casey Cruse, Lois Dalzell, Liana Davila, Dolf de Roos, Ph.D., Jennifer Fair, Deborah Fine, Abbey Fleck, Kristina Garabedian, Neale Godfrey, Brian Griese, Mark Victor Hansen, Gideon Hill, Beverly & Elwood Johnson, Dennis & Donna Johnson, Stan & Julie Johnson, Ben Kaplan, Kauffman Foundation, Kids Hall of Fame, KidsWay, Robert T. Kiyosaki, Jeff Koon, Phillip Lechter, Sharon Lechter, Mel Levine, Tim & Sheri Lindquist, Mary Katherine Lindsay, Elsie and Evan Macmillan, Dave Mantel, Roddy and Judy Meadows, Cecy Mets, Annette & Steve Mills, Melanie Moen, Victoria Nesnick, Sean, Brendan and Paddy O'Connell, Andy Powell, Margaret Rhyne, Doreen Sederquist, Dr. Laura Schlessinger, Willard Stawski II, Cheryl Stoker, Michele Stutz, Therese Tiab, Larry Vergun, Teresa Walker, Walt Disney Co., Bruce Williams, Tiger Woods, Robert Wynn, A. J. Yager, Zig Zigler.

About the Authors

● ●

Sheri Provost

SHERI PROVOST and **LISA JORDAN,** who are still kids at heart, were born and raised in California. They pride themselves on being mavericks: they have never been ones to follow the herd. Each author has years of experience in business, accounting, consulting and sales, and both are currently successful entrepreneurs and writers.

The reality of CashCow Kids™ came about when the authors realized most people don't start learning about money until later in life. Their mission is to lead the way in educating both children and parents in the field of family financial literacy. They know the road to prosperity begins at home and can be set upon at virtually any age.

Both authors live in the lush green pastures of central California where they are busy raising their own CashCow Kids™.

Lisa Jordan

Permissions

• •

We would like to acknowledge the following publishers and individuals for permission to print the following material. (Note: The stories that were penned anonymously, that are public domain or were written by Lisa Jordan or Sheri Provost are not included in this listing.)

Abbey Fleck, Makin Bacon. Printed with permission of Jon Fleck, Young Biz, and The Kauffman Foundation.

AJ Yager, LifeForce, Smart™Grandparenting. Printed with permission of AJ Yager, Life Force Enterprises, and Smartgrandparenting.

Ben Kaplan, Scholarship Coach. Printed with permission of Ben Kaplan.

Brian Griese, Judith Ann Griese Foundation. Printed with permission of Brian Griese and the Judith Ann Griese Foundation.

Christopher Haas. Printed with permission of Christopher Haas Enterprises, Young Biz, and The COSTCO Connection.

David Adamiec, Kids Packs USA. Printed with permission of David Adamiec.

Dolf de Roos, Ph.D. Printed with permission of Dolf de Roos, Ph.D., Property Prosperity.

Elise and Evan Macmillan, The Chocolate Farm. Printed with permission of Kathleen Macmillan, The Chocolate Farm and The COSTCO Connection.

Jeff Koon and Andy Powell, You May Not Tie an Alligaror to a Fire Hydrant. Printed with permission of Jeff Koon and Andy Powell, The Free Press, a Division of Simon & Schuster.

Kristina Garabedian, Shoe Box Giving. Printed with permission of Robert L. Garabedian.

Kyle and Ian Amber, Kids That Care. Printed with permission of Laurie Amber, Kids That Care Pediatric and Cancer Fund.

Mary Catherine Lindsay, Grasshopper Press. Printed with permission of Dana M. Lindsay and The COSTCO Connection.

Olivia Bennett. A Life in Full Bloom. Printed with permission of Ben Valenty.

One Minute Millionaire by Mark Victor Hansen and Robert G. Allen. Printed with permission of One Minute Millionaire, LLC.

Rich Dad Books, CASHFLOW for Kids™, CASHFLOW 101®, Straight Talk Newsletter. Printed by permission of CASHFLOW Technologies, and The Rich Dad Company.

Richard K. Anderson Jr. (excerpt from article " Money, Power, Respect: Keeping It Real for the Kids.") Printed with permission of Richard K. Anderson Sr., Africana.com and Carolyn M. Brown, author and columnist.

The Complete Cow by Sara Rath. Reprinted by permission of Voyageur Press, Inc., Stillwater, MN.

The Man Nobody Knows by Bruce Barton. Reprinted with permission of Simon & Schuster.

The O'Connell Brothers. Printed with permission of The O'Connell brothers, Young Biz and The Kauffman Foundation. Adapted from *Y & E The Magazine for Teen Entrepreneurs* — May/June 2000 ©2000 Ewing Marion Kauffman Foundation and KidsWay, Inc. All rights reserved.

Walt Disney Company and Disney Enterprises, Inc. This book makes reference to various Disney copyrighted characters, trademarks, marks and registered marks owned by The Walt Disney Company and Disney Enterprises, Inc.

Index

ABACUS PUBLISHING

Quick Order Form

Fax orders:	(559) 298-8304 Send this form.
Telephone orders:	(866) MOO-LAAH toll free (866-666-5224) Have your credit card ready.
E-Mail orders:	orders@cashcowkids.com
Postal orders:	CashCow Kids 2930 Geer Road, Suite 174 Turlock, CA 95382

Please send the following:

___CashCow Kids™ (book)	$19.95	$_____
___CashCow Kids™ (CD/audio)	$24.95	$_____
___CashCow Bank	$19.95	$_____
___Have a CashCow Kit	$39.95	$_____

(All prices subject to change.)

Sales Tax (California residents) $_____

Shipping by air: U.S.: $4.00 for first product
$2.00 for each additional product   Shipping $_____
TOTAL $_____

Please send order to:

Name: _____

Address: _____

City: _____ State: _____ Zip: _____

Telephone: _____

E-mail address: _____

Please send me FREE information on:
___Other books ___Speaking/seminars ___Other Products

Method of Payment:
___Visa   ___Mastercard   ___AMEX   ___Discover

Card number: _____

Name on card: _____ Exp. Date: _____

www.cashcowkids.com

www.cashcowkids.com

N E